Foreword by BA

Dropping Almonds was first published in 2008. 2008 was also a year the US government nearly defaulted on its currency due to bad mortgages and poor lending practices by financial institutions. Nobody went to Federal prison over the mortgage crisis and the banks still hold American citizens hostage for their own poor judgment. In the Fall of 2008, the United States elected its first African American as President. Even though I thought Barrack Hussein Obama was charismatic and an excellent speaker, I didn't vote for him. My vote had nothing to do with race, but everything to do with experience. I didn't believe that Obama had the experience necessary to deal with the magnitude of problems facing the United States. No doubt the US changed dramatically after the events of September 11, 2001. I doubt that George W Bush anticipated much of his Presidency would be preoccupied with preventing future attacks on our homeland and pursuing terrorists in a faraway, unpredictable land.

2008 was a year that most people remember because of the impact to life savings and retirement accounts. From October 2007 to the beginning of 2009, the stock market of the Dow Jones Industrial Average had lost over 50% of its value. Many of our seniors had to go back to work to pay for the damage done to their retirement accounts. The seniors were also competing with freshly graduated college students that were looking for careers. There are several parallels between the stock market crash of 1929 and the subsequent crash that occurred from 2008-2009. Times were tough in 2008, and wages are still impacted by a slow recovery today.

Dropping Almonds was written as a lesson in business from the perspective of a Vice President with a multi-hundred million-dollar company. Not your "typical" business book with quotes, lessons, and motivating ideas, Dropping Almonds is raw and emotional. The book captures how convoluted and confused the upper echelons of some organizations are managed. You won't find your cheese, many of the elements go from bad to worse, and the story doesn't have a happy ending. However, the book is about the realities of business.

A person that reviewed the book stated there are two sides to a story and I was only telling one side. I disagree. There are three sides to every story: Theirs, Mine, and the **Truth**. A reference was also made to getting beyond the personal pain of the author to find nuggets of value. The opinion of the reviewer is spot on. However, the way we relate to each other in business says a lot about the way we lead our lives. Laying off employees, closing stores, and upending people's lives has a profound affect on our Self.

Self, or our sense of it, has significant meaning in our lives according to therapists, especially psychoanalysts. For those that have read the work of Sigmund Freud and other psychopioneers, the ego has no sense of right or wrong. Hence, the egomaniacs in a workplace focus on satisfying their needs by any means necessary. We know them. They're climbing all over everyone else to satisfy their egos. On the other hand, we have employees that are trying to achieve an ideal sense of self. They see themselves more like they ought to be: in a career, in a family, as a parent, or with their friends. These people are better defined as those with conscience. When employees have a sense of self, and don't see themselves doing the things they set out to accomplish (goals), conflict emerges. Those who aren't able to achieve their ideal self, have a strong sense of guilt.

I'm not sure why Corporate America doesn't incorporate more psychology into management techniques. People are different and have different needs, not everyone is motivated by money. Some employees might be happy with additional days off or tickets to a special venue. At the lowest level, behavioral techniques of reward and punishment are usually applied by supervisors that have very little training to do so. In most organizations, reviews are done once a year in haste. Most supervisors have too many direct reports and they are more focused on getting a review process over with than making it meaningful to employees. Quality, not quantity!

The sequel to Dropping Almonds will be released this year (2015). So much has happened during the past seven years! So much to learn and so little time. Because of the sting associated with my experience, I needed to let Dropping Almonds sit on the shelf…for years. I was upset when I wrote the first installation for a number of reasons. Life, and more importantly, time has a way of taking care of things. This edition of Dropping Almonds has been edited very little to maintain the essence of what I was thinking when putting the chapters together.

For the reader, there are some bad words and poop references. If you don't like seeing those in print, you may want to pass on this piece of literary work. This is my side of the story, I hope you enjoy the pages and embrace some of the lessons I learned. Stay tuned for a follow up to Dropping Almonds.

Dropping Almonds is intended as a general guide to the topics discussed. It is not intended and should not be used as a substitute for professional advice (medical, legal, or otherwise) and the reader is advised to seek independent, professional advice.

Although every precaution has been taken to verify the accuracy of the information contained herein, the author and publisher assume no responsibility for any errors or omissions. No liability is assumed for damages that may result from the use of information contained herein. Additionally, this is a work in the nature of a memoir, not a work of journalism; the interchanges with the people portrayed herein are the recreation of the author's own emotions and memory.

All rights reserved. No part of this publication may be reproduced or transmitted without the written prior permission of the author.

Thanks to **Nuts For Life** for the Almonds Image.
www.nutsforlife.com.au

A Gigs-N-Rigs Production, 2014

Let the games begin...

No preface, no introductions, nada...by the way, who isn't thankful for their parents? If it weren't for them, you wouldn't be reading this. So, what is the purpose of Dropping Almonds? Why spend the time writing a novel to help educate employees about cutthroat politics of the business world, not to forget, their own employers? Why is my story different or unique, and why should you take the time to read something like this? My story is not really different from the millions of Associates that enter the business world to find themselves somewhat lost and disillusioned by what they see and hear. Why should you take the time to read Dropping Almonds? Perhaps it may help you understand your place in the business world, life, or in a family. My story is unique, to a degree, because it's mine. But what's really ours anyway????????

The concept of Dropping Almonds. We have all dropped almonds at some point in our lives and it's a painful process. Put yourself in a position to think back and imagine a setting. Now, remember a time when you were terribly constipated, possibly after Thanksgiving, a good night of drinking, or a wedding reception. You're literally full of shit but don't know if a trip to the vitreous china will help relieve your excesses. So you think things out: reading material, toilet paper on the roll, a DVD playing for the kids downstairs, and you retreat to a very personal place to manufacture a product. Shit is a manufactured product by the way. There are several components that go into making shit, both external and internal. Infeed and outfeed are terms utilized in the manufacturing world and your body is no different. However, because of complex processes and organs that must work as a team, your night of frolicking and making an idiot out of yourself disrupts the process. Essentially, you don't know if your organs will bear fruit because your piping isn't quite functioning like it should. Piping can also be affected by stress, physical ailments, dehydration, and a host of other issues too many to mention here.

Let me digress a little. Freud was very much into the anal stage of psyche development. I studied this extensively during college and believe that Freud was either onto something or very impressed with his own doody. Most people are very impressed with their own shit and, in many cases, want to share it with others. This is no different than the business world and the shit that gets shoveled around on a daily basis. People talk shit, write shit, goof up and think "Oh shit", or think they're the shit. So while Freud considered the anal stage a very early stage of psyche development, children have a tendency to take their shit with them, and if they're really lucky, they'll take some of their parents too. Anywho...I digress and apologize. Back to our constipated person...

So, there you are, pants at the ankles with the window open or fan on. Your magazine, book, or junk mail is in hand to help you endure the time constipation will spend for you. Your bowels begin to grumble and funny, squishy noises emanate from your mid-section. If you're really lucky, you'll feel some pain in the lower abdomen or rectum. After about three minutes of body gyrations and sweat beginning to protrude from your cheeks (butt) and forehead, you lose the reading material and assume the concentration of Tiger Woods at the British Open. Now you're determined. Determined to move whatever this is out of your body. You push; you grab the toilet seat in anticipation that your ass may explode. You may even try Lamaze breathing techniques to ease the bowels and move the shit out of you. None of that works. Now you're pushing at three-second intervals to pinch a loaf. Wait a minute...what's that? A turtlehead. Ooops, there it goes, it just retreated back into the rectum. Push again and there she is; however, every time I do this that little turd retreats!!!! Now I'm pushing with a blood pressure of 250/125. I'm probably on the verge of cardiac arrest, a stroke, tearing my asshole to shreds, but I don't care. This piece of shit is coming out of my ass, even if it means permanent hemorrhoids. After pushing so hard that you see stars, you finally hear a tiny "ker-plunk". When you first started this expedition, you thought you'd take the biggest dump ever and feel fantastic. After seven to ten minutes of some of the hardest childbirth type pushing (guys-----I'm taking some latitude here), you look down into the toilet and see an almond. Instant disappointment comes over you and you can't believe that you've labored to the point of exhaustion to manufacture an almond. **All of that work for so little return**.

I have manufactured many almonds in the business world over the past several years. I am the product of a Cinderella story that turned into a pumpkin, or egg on my face. I have heard all of the great thinkers of the business world discuss Visions, Missions, Values, Vertically Integrated Solutions, Who has the "D"?, Who's on first, What's on second, concentric circles, <u>Crucial Conversations</u>, <u>Crucial Confrontations</u>, Strategery, <u>The Five Dysfunctions of a Team</u>, Boulders and Big Rocks, Bedrock, Hard Rock, Kid Rock, blah, blah, blah, blah, and blah. I'm so sick and tired of the American Dream or the thought of trying to attain it. Most Associates, at any level of an organization, are out for themselves...period. Being selfish at the basement levels of a company is not all that bad, unless Associates are stealing from you; but being selfish at the upper levels of a company can be catastrophic. I worked for a company that doesn't have a woman at the executive level. There used to be one, but she wasn't a good fit for the organization and eventually moved on. Two families that acted as operators within the organization owned the company. At upper levels of the organization, the division between families was evident. At basement levels of the organization, things just appeared to be fucked up and Associates didn't really understand the politics involved at the tip of the iceberg. I served in this environment for 2 1/2 years as the VICE PRESIDENT of the BLUNDERLAND REGION and became very familiar with dropping almonds and people getting in the way of progress (see map at back of book).

ESTABLISHING CREDIBILITY

So why me? Why should you listen to me? Who is Bach Anon and why should you care? Pretty simple and some of this logic dates back to the beginning of civilization. It doesn't matter what my title is, how much education I've received, whether or not I'm good at Trivial Pursuit, or anything that can be tied to first-person statements. JUST DO WHAT I SAY I'M GOING TO DO. Don't lie about things, don't try and elevate a sometimes crappy performance on a project...just be honest. There is so much dishonesty in the marketplace today that a norm has been established. Most people will assume that you're just bullshitting them and it's their job to establish the truth. People make commitments today and don't give a shit whether or not they're met or executed. I remember the first executive meeting I attended a couple of years back. There were some questions that popped up and answers weren't readily available. An executive leader of the company stated that we would put the questions in the "parking lot" and a commitment was made to follow up on the questions that had been tabled. Two and a half years later, I'm still waiting for answers. I'm not sure if the leader thought Associates would forget, that the items didn't really matter, or that he didn't owe us explanations. The point is, he made a commitment and didn't follow-up. Taboo! If you don't remember anything else from this book, which you probably won't, remember this: **Don't skate on YOUR commitments**.

What separates me from the pack? I always did what I said I was going to do. Even if I sometimes failed or made a mistake, I always acknowledged the commitment I made and stuck to it. A lack of credibility is rampant in the business world today. Do you know why people read books about time management, building teams, setting goals, or becoming better leaders? They lack confidence in their own abilities. So, instead of bucking up and stating, "Hey, I don't know what the fuck I'm doing and I need help from my team," most leaders hide behind this aura of impenetrable power and super-hero confidence. I used to love it when I'd pose a question to a fellow peer, senior leader and they would become perplexed because they didn't have the answer. They would ask me what I would do. I would go through the steps of how I would implement a solution to the problem and there would be silence on the phone. After what seemed like a long, uncomfortable silence (something I've learned to become comfortable with), the fellow on the other end would shoot the idea down or spin the idea a different way. This used to piss me off to no end. I knew, and my peer knew, they didn't know what the fuck they were doing; however, they would shoot ideas down or become spin-doctors to make themselves feel like they were contributing at some level to the organization. Any of this sound familiar? Get over yourself already! You're at the top of the organization and wage earners depend on your ability to step back or step forward, and in some cases, stepping down.

Even in the midst of my recent demotion (somewhat forced, somewhat voluntary), my boss told all of my direct reports that "...he did nothing wrong", that "...he had always done what he was instructed to do." As I'm sitting there with my direct reports, Associates that I value/cherish deeply in my position, I'm thinking, "Why in the fuck am I being demoted?" Why isn't the person who was giving me direction being held accountable? Why am I the fall guy? To be completely honest, I was so sick and tired of the bullshit and almond dropping I had done as a Vice President that I welcomed the demotion. The executives higher than me needed to feel good about their contributions to the organization, much like reading their stupid fucking books, so they targeted the youngest, least tenured executive on the team: ME. That whole story is for a different section later in the book. I remember the former VP of the Blunderland Region, the guy I replaced, used to phone me up while I was the General Manager of our North Pole location. We didn't have much business to speak of and there weren't many opportunities for us to conquer. He used to ask me, "What's coming down the pike?" I would respond "nothing" and explain that our image, inadequate sales team, and previous problems from previous ownership were going to be very difficult to overcome. We would need a serious amount of time to overcome our obstacles and put the right team in place. I remember the absolute silence on the other end of the line. You could have heard a pin drop in the next county because of the phone's silence. Then a canned response of, "Keep plugging away" or "Keep the team busy" would follow the prolonged silence. **Sidebar: When you're a supervisor in charge of Associates, don't ever provide canned responses that are shallow and lack substance. You're better off not saying anything or at least acknowledging how difficult a task or struggle may be.**

Later on that same VP told me how he always valued my honest responses to him and how the responses allowed him to better assess the situation. What was I going to do? Lie? Tell him something that wasn't true and look like an ass to the company and my boss later on. The market, at least our performance, in the North Pole stunk! He knew it, I knew it, the Associates knew it, and everyone knew it. Now that I look back on the question, I think, "What a dumb question." After eight months in the North Pole, the VP who valued my honest opinions pulled me from the branch and consolidated our Nolava operation into the North Pole. Several associates were severed, or RIFed (Reduction In Force) to move forward with a stronger, more powerful branch. I remember sitting down with my boss, the VP dude I mentioned earlier. He sat me down and stated that "...I've made a decision." He proceeds to tell me that he's consolidating the markets and that I will no longer be the General Manager of the North Pole location. Then there was a real long pause and the VP just stared at me. I don't know if he was expecting me to get pissed, to fly off the handle, to whoop his ass, I just don't know. But I let the silence play out and I didn't say a thing. I remember my father telling me a long time ago, "He who speaks first loses." I had lost the battle but I wasn't going to surrender the war. The VP finally breaks the silence and says, "Do you want to stay with the company?" I looked at him kinda funny, with the tired eyes of a manager who'd put too much time in over the past several months, and stated, "Well so-and-so, I believe that I hired on with a company and not just a branch, of course I want to remain with the company." In the back of my mind I'm thinking..."I just finished the first successful physical inventory of that branch's short history with the company and I'm being moved out." I took inventory on Saturday/Sunday and was asked to leave on Monday; I was glad to be pulled out of that branch should the truth be told. To this day, the branch has not been successful, and because of the current housing market (2007-2008), will likely see poorer days ahead. Good people...bad business model and poor executive decision making from my perspective.

I was diagnosed Obsessive-Compulsive early on in life. I saw a Psychiatrist for several years of my adolescence and worked hard to work through a very debilitating condition. One thing I learned about people that are obsessive-compulsive is that they have a very high regard for good/evil, Jesus/devil, black/white, and an overall high moral structure. Most of what I feared was retribution from a God that was not happy with what I was doing or how I was conducting myself. I believed that if I didn't perform certain rituals: touching door-knobs, counting and touching items, kicking the underside of people's shoes, that God was going to punish me or the devil was going to possess me. While the issues I just described seem like they're surreal or from a mental hospital transcription, they were very real and inescapable to me at the time. This was a very, very, very dark period in my life. I can remember lying in bed hoping that God would take me because I couldn't imagine living the rest of my life like this. Every single minute of every single day was occupied with counting, touching, and praying that the Lord would spare me and my family from evil and bad things that happen in the world. Talk about dropping almonds. I was wound up tighter than a rubber band powered propeller on a kid's old fashioned wooden plane...Git-R-Done (Larry the Cable Guy). Thankfully, my parents, shrink, and friends helped me through this period and I eventually let go of my demons (literally). So, what's born out of something bad must come something good...or so they say. **Sidebar: For those of you reading this book that have suffered from symptoms of OCD, regardless of severity, I feel your pain and understand your demons.**

I was taught to use my OCD in more positive fashions. Focus energy on studying, playing guitar, and excelling at whatever I did. While my beliefs changed, my personality did not; I was more inclined to use the debilitation as a propellant to get things done and succeed in life. While some of this has toned down over the past several years, some of it is still very much alive and helping me to remain morally vigilant. I have a strong sense of who I am and what I can contribute to a team, as long as we don't color outside the lines.

COLORING OUTSIDE THE LINES

My first "real" job was with PC in 1993. I had just graduated from Texas Tech University and was hungry to get out into the real world. With my Psychology degree and minor in English, I was ready to fix the world and do it in such a way that people could understand. I was so naive at the time. I thought there was big money coming from business and that I would be set because I had a degree. I'll never forget the interview I had with a record company on the Tech campus. There were two ladies and a gentleman to represent the company and conduct interviews. I remember seeing the sign-up sheet for interviews and was a little intimidated that MBA, Finance, Accounting, and other Graduate majors were interviewing with the record company. This was a record company wasn't it? Was I under-qualified with a psych degree? The competition was pretty fierce, but I was the Treasurer and President of my fraternity with a long history of good grades. The Dean and President's Lists were emblazoned with my name for the past four years. I was ready to take on the world one CD at a time...

The interview was the toughest experience I'd had in college. One of the women was pregnant and I thought she may show some compassion, but she was as relentless as the other two. They began to grill me and I started sweating. Instead of focusing on my accomplishments and what I could bring to their business, they focused on everything I didn't have. Why wasn't I a business major? Why didn't I want to stay in the field of psychology and pursue graduate school? What made me better than some of the masters' students interviewing for the entry-level position? I had very confused, nervous responses that convinced them that I was not made out for the CD business. I walked out of that interview pissed and drenched. They treated me like some kind of second-rate flunky that couldn't handle the business world. To this day, I haven't bought a thing from that record company either. I was so unimpressed with the way they treated me, I figured they might treat their clients the same way. I can understand if someone believes that I lack the qualifications to handle a position, but let me know up front so we don't waste everyone's time. I was so pissed that I went out and bought a book on how to interview. I forgot which book it was, but the book provided me some of the best advice I've received from the self-help genre of getting/keeping a job. The book stated that if an interviewer(s) focused on your weaknesses more so than your strengths, politely get up, thank the interviewer for their time, and explain that it appears you don't seem to be the right fit for their company. Don't waste your time, their time, or the office time to be awarded a job you have no chance of getting. I'm sure several of you have been in the same situation. You leave pissed off, hating the interviewer, and vowing to never step foot in that office again. I admit that it's embarrassing, but don't waste your energy on supervisors that don't know how to interview or value a person in their presence. They need to step off their pedestals, see the true value of people in front of them, and open their perspectives beyond just what they know. Many supervisors and managers of companies miss the boat with seeing, and maintaining, the value of Associates.

The company I worked for had a Vision statement that touted the importance of Associates making contributions to client's needs. The Vision statement should be reworked to state something that is more representative of what this company, and many others do, "...Associates play an important role to the company as long as profits rise and FTE productivity stays strong; should profits dip and FTE productivity decline because of market conditions, YOU'RE ON YOUR OWN." I met with my boss in late January/early February of this year (2007) and we had a very tough conversation. He had been meeting with a consultant/coach and wanted to try out some of his new accountability vernacular. Therefore, he sat me down and developed a very serious tone. He summed up how the Blunderland Region had performed over the past several years, even prior to my arrival, and cautiously stated that if results didn't change, he was going to look to make a change.

At that point I had the weirdest physical sensation in my life. My heart got very hot, almost to the point of boiling and I damn near came out of my chair. Now, while I can't spell out all of the nitty-gritty, dirty details of the horse-shit, almond dropping stuff I'd been through in the past 2 years right here, I experienced the deepest sense of disappointment I'd ever felt. As the Vice President of Blunderdland, I had poured my heart and soul into the performance of the Region. While profits had suffered under my leadership, there were several reasons why. Think about rebuilding a football team to become a better club. The front office is typically restructured, players are waived or hit the free agency market, coaches are excused, and turmoil sets in. In the head coach's mind (my mind), amidst the chaos, there was a plan to rebuild the organization from the bottom up and be a contender for the post season. Sometimes it works, sometimes it doesn't. However, goals and strategies take months, years, and decades to play out. A rule of thumb that you can use to manage your career and business is the following: **It will take you twice as long to fix things than to keep them right or from derailing**. For instance, if a bad manager, sales rep, ops manager is in place and the general population of Associates or clients considers them a poor performer, you must get rid of them immediately. If you let them stumble along for a year while you're hoping they improve, it will take you two years to clean up their almonds; you'll be dropping your own during the cleanup stage. If you let them go two years and perform poorly, give yourself about four years of cleanup. The higher the position, the more difficult it is to clean up people's problems in double the time of their tenure. Depending on how severe people are allowed to screw up the operations/logistics of a company, the company may never recover. Don't forget, clients and distributors have several options in the marketplace, and they're not going to drop almonds for very long to carry you along (individually or as a team). I digress, back to the story...

So, I begin the Vice President, Regional Operations Manager for Blunderland in January/February of 2005. I knew that I was in trouble right out of the gate. Knowing what I know now, I would have remained in the beautiful Enchanted Desert and continued to run the small showroom/lumberyard operation I had spent the past two years managing. At the very beginning of our transition, the outgoing VP asked me if I was made aware of all the changes coming down the pike. Somewhat befuddled I responded, "no". Then the outgoing VP proceeded to tell me how I was going to need to sell off the location in Barnia mid-year, announce the closing of the Nevercan facility by year end, and prepare for the terminations of existing leases by the end of 2006. At no point did my boss give me any indication that so much was on the horizon and that I wouldn't have time to get my feet wet. At no time did the outgoing VP give me any indication, during the interviewing process, that he would leave me such a big bag of trials. Why would he? Thinking back, he was, in my opinion, burned out by the position, hadn't visited his branches very frequently, and was always involved in the greater "greatness" of running the company. Nice to know that I would be spending the first year and a half of my tenure as a VP explaining to Associates they would be out of work and trying to convince our clients to move their business to other locations. I now have the opinion that corporate gurus, private owners, and anyone else that hasn't been an operator has absolutely zero sense of how much work and effort it takes to roll a 200# boulder up a fourteener. I wasn't prepared to handle the issues in front of me, but I'd give it a yeoman's try.

At the same time I was interviewing for the VP position, I was/am/whatever, diagnosed with heart disease. I could tell something was wrong at the beginning of 2004. I would sometimes feel light-headed and my heart would skip beats or pound. I believe the damage was done back in 2001 when I was serving as a General Manager Trainee for a company I worked for. I remember being sick and running a fever. Because I was a macho-man dumb ass, I believed that being sick shouldn't prevent me from working. I downed cold medicine and did my best to get everyone else sick at the office. At around quitting time, I noticed that my heart began to pound. I figured that I must have OD'd on the cold medicine and shook the first few abnormal beats off. I tried to carry on conversations with the guys up front, but excused myself, rather rapidly, after I realized that my heart was just beginning to pound. Who wants to die, in their early 30's, in front of a bunch of friends/co-workers? I figured that I would do the safe, less embarrassing thing, and drive home to die. To avoid embarrassment, I would have preferred to die in my vehicle and risk the lives of others to get home. Not very bright as I look back on things. I called my wife and told her that I was having a heart attack or something like it. She encouraged me to call 911, but I believed that I could make it home to croak if that was the case. My heart raced and pounded all the way home. Once I arrived, my wife had me call the doctor/hospital to explain my condition. I was gulping water to try and re-hydrate my body from the fever and sweats produced during the day. The nurse talked me through some symptoms and remedies to calm me down. She referred me to visit the Urgent Care facility the next day to have an EKG recorded and read. The EKG showed no abnormal heartbeats or damage from a heart attack. So, I went about my merry way and thought everything was fine. I mean, everything is fine when a doctor tells you it's fine, right???? **Sidebar: Anyone fortunate enough to read this book will be fortunate enough to experience trials today, tomorrow, and in the future. Trials define our soul, character, and dynamics in family. Don't be upset that you've been chosen to experience life's trials, but be diligent to examine the source of the trials and why you've been chosen. My heart disease is one of several trials in life...**

On the day I was to phone my future boss and follow-up with my interest level in the VP position, essentially set up an interview, I was having a trachea-echo performed on my heart. Even though I went through the stress test, the doctor wanted to see some close ups of my valves functioning. I had never been through a trachea-echo and the doctor made it seem like the procedure was a piece of cake. Take some funny juice via IV and the doctor would put a small tube with a camera down my throat. Nothing was mentioned about numbing my throat beforehand to kill the gag reflex prior to the procedure. I gagged, and gagged, and gagged, and gagged as the nurse attempted to get my throat numb. They kept numbing my throat, or trying, and I kept gagging. I don't think my gag reflex ever went away because they were still spraying numbing agents as they administered the goofy juice. The poor gal that had to endure my gagging, spewing, and eyes watering. I made the mistake of asking her what was behind the bed sheet on the wall. She said that it was the apparatus used to take pictures. I said that I wanted to see it. She removed the sheet and there was a garden hose with a camera attached. The garden hose was about five feet long and there was a very small optical device on the end of it. How awful it must be on the other side of torture, especially when you don't want to torture the patients you're working with. A few days after the procedure I bought the nurse a card and thanked her for her patience and tolerance with me. I had to phone the outgoing VP and let him know that I was in no position to speak to my future boss and had undergone a procedure that left my voice raspy. After that, I had to sit down with the VP and let him know about my health and some of the personal obstacles facing me in the next couple of weeks, years, decades (God willing). As a side note, I have the best cardiologist in the world and an exceptional staff serves him.

I remember the conversation with the VP like it was yesterday. I mean, he had selfish motives and wanted to move on for obvious reasons (burnout, boredom, promotion, and whatever other undisclosed reasons). He actually looked at me and asked, "Does stress cause your heart condition?" I looked at him, kinda perplexed, and stated, "Well, I asked the doctor and he said that while stress is likely not the cause, it sure doesn't help the condition". The VP then asked me what happens if it got worse and presumptuously queried, "Would they put in a pacemaker to fix it?" While I didn't pretend to be a doctor, I informed the VP that other procedures would probably be required to prevent heart failure. The VP exhibited what appeared to be general concern, but then again, he was/is good at "acting" with compassion (my opinion). In reality and looking back, the company had tried to fill the VP position with a couple of other high caliber Associates from other regions for several months. I was probably the third or fourth candidate on the list. I'm sure that everyone, including the outgoing VP, were a little worn out by the process and looked to fill the position rapidly. Not to mention, the Region was setting up for the perfect storm, as a member of Marketing had so eloquently described in a later conversation with me. The Blunderland Region was doomed and there was little I could do to prevent the turmoil. However, in light of all the almonds, and the turmoil on the horizon, nobody mentioned a word to me. I would have figured that after my recent health developments, they would have at least been honest with me about the professional obstacles ahead. Selling a position can sometimes take on the appearance of being sold a used car. Pat my back, put me in the car, and have me drive away, only to break down 3 miles away. **Sidebar: I broke down well before I reached the 3 mile mark.**

When I interviewed with my future boss, my heartbeat was irregular the whole time. Some of this was nerves, some of it was exhaustion, and some of it was my body trying to blow the interview. It's funny how animals/insects can anticipate future events. Maybe we as humans, through some level of pre-cognition, can also detect danger before it happens. I didn't feel relaxed in the interview and felt out of my element. I interviewed and listened well, but I felt like I was out of sorts. I wasn't very good at bullshitting, and most senior leaders admired that quality about me, even though it cost me the position down the road. <u>Remember, people at all levels admire and will follow someone that tells the truth, even to their demise, or martyrdom.</u> Look at how many companies, across this great nation and globe, have fallen at the hands of their own egotistical leadership. Mismanagement of finances, scandals, mortgage crisis, etc., etc., etc. Egos and people wanting to line their own pockets bring many of these problems about. The government does it as well. Just consider, for a moment, how many billions/trillions of dollars are pulled from the economy to finance bad government. Government scandal is the largest contemporary problem of the millennium, even bigger than climate change. Government will likely succeed in killing off humanity long before climate change. No doubt that climate change is a problem that needs to be solved and reversed if possible, but government scandal is a crisis, and we pay our hard earned money to finance it. The beauty of Rush Limbaugh and his radio show is that his radio nation feeds off the predictability that the government will fuck up, especially focusing on Democrats, and they'll have something to talk about tomorrow. Without scandal, there would be no Rush, and he would have to resort to other content for his radio show. If a scandal doesn't exist, just make one up. We need to sell more papers and have more listeners!

ONWARD AND BACKWARD

I was named Vice President of the Blunderland Region in January of 2005. The task was going to be difficult for a number of reasons. I wasn't political and didn't know how to play the game. The tasks in front of me were much bigger than what I could handle. I was also named a VP in the Region I had called home since 2001. There were going to be peer issues and posturing, perhaps, from those who felt I wasn't qualified to handle the tasks in front of me. Little did they know that I was on their side. I didn't believe that I possessed the skills or experience to make a good run at the position. I knew that I would have to partner with Managers in the field to maintain, or God forbid, improve status quo. Financially we were going to be screwed in the Region for the next couple of years, but I possessed some people skills that would help me build, and maintain, a good team. Thank goodness I had completed some graduate work in counseling and done an internship at a counseling center in the town I reside. After counseling individuals, couples, families, professionals, and kids, I learned a few tricks about how to handle people and myself.

I dropped my first almond in Barnia. Shortly after accepting the new position, I began to prepare for the sale of the company's Barnia branch. The branch wasn't a poor or stellar performer; it just didn't meet the Vision and long-term direction of the company. Remember this line, as you will hear it over and over and over and over as you progress through your own career. The great thinkers, the almond infeeders, the grand Pooh-Bahs of higher knowledge love to say, "...the design did not fit the model of our company." Even if the design makes money, even if the design shows promise, it doesn't matter. Many of your days producing almonds will be fighting for the greater good of the company, because internally, intellectually, inferentially, the Vision and higher thinking doesn't make sense at the field level. I remember attending a strategic meeting for the company I worked for and heard a VP say that as a strategic company, "...we must learn to decide what we're not going to do first." So, what did we do? We began to limit our offerings, limit our client base, and become more linear in our thought processes and the services we would provide. We were going to become strategic, even if it meant that we would tell certain clients that we were no longer interested in serving their needs. This was quite contrary to what I'd learned in business before. I learned that you not only graciously received the dollar that was being offered for services, but you found out ways to receive more dollars and say "thank you". Revenues were strong during these strategic times and the company felt confident about writing off some client segments, especially the ones that yielded very good margins. We were beginning to look more and more like everyone else, and there wasn't much that differentiated us from the competition, even though we claimed it was our service.

That's what's great about the airline industry. Pricing is pretty much the same across the board, so look at airlines that have improved over the past couple of years. Southwest Airlines has always been strong and Herb Kelleher has a very strong commitment to the Associates. Frontier Airlines, the one I'm most familiar with, has very good attendants and the pilots thank travelers for keeping them employed. However, look at American and Delta. I can't speak for Delta directly, but I flew American tons while traveling back to corporate headquarters to become educated about the ways of lumber business. Lumber is a commodity, much like the airline industry, and service will truly separate the men from the boys, women from the girls, leaders from followers...you get the point. I quit flying American because some attendants "generally" didn't like their jobs. They were performing the job because they wanted to travel, or they wanted time off, not because they liked American. In my opinion, some attendants were very angry with American and felt that their pensions (or whatever) were unfairly cut and that there was no future with American. I began to rationalize to myself...okay, if the attendants feel this way, then the pilots probably aren't happy...if the pilots aren't happy, then the mechanics probably aren't happy (they strike all the time anyway, don't they?), and I quit flying American. A bunch of money moved from American to Frontier because of the people; I drove farther from point A to point B to fly Frontier. Bottom line: if you don't take care of the people, even when you claim you do, your clients will move elsewhere, period. They should! More people should vote with their money and more bad businesses would become extinct. If a company states that they're employee oriented, and they cut employees at the first sign of trouble, what does that tell you? If you're in with a company that has poor service and doesn't take care of their Associates, find another employer. The business world needs more natural selection and less Divine intervention. In my opinion, the lumber company I worked for used to be employee oriented. Most Associates used to feel like they were part of the family. Several Associates began to walk around like zombies wandering from morning to afternoon. Not knowing whether or not our contributions meant something to somebody, we dropped almonds.

Back to Barnia...I was instructed to meet with the new owners, schedule an inventory, and prepare an announcement for the Associates that were being sold. Associates are really just another asset, or liability depending on how you look at them, to the income statement. From my earlier assessments and opinions, Southwest Airlines...asset, American Airlines...liability. Same dollars and very similar people, the difference is in how they're treated. Associates in Barnia...liability to the company and not part of the Vision. I did all of the prep work that was required and met with the Manager by phone and in person to develop a game plan. I very much like(d) the Manager of Barnia and thought he did a very good job. He was going to remain with the company and transfer to our Can'tasia location, after due diligence and post close were performed for the sale, to become a middle manager. Everything went well until the meeting. I, we, completely caught the Associates off guard and there was utter shock. One of our Associates had to excuse herself because she couldn't believe the message. Then I proceeded to tell the Associates about what would happen to their accrued and earned vacation, how we would handle their 401k, when their benefits would expire, when the new owner planned to take over, and went on and on about the logistics behind the sale. The Associates didn't hear me after I said, "Sold". They were more concerned about their positions, their car payments, their medical expenses, etc.... They felt abandoned and I could see it in their faces. Right after I gave my demotivating speech, my heartbeat went irregular, very irregular. I felt fatigued, exhausted, and like I was going to pass out. I'm not sure how I made it through the question/answer portion of the meeting. I began sweating, I felt like I was making a poor decision for the company by being there. I felt ashamed to be their leader and believed that I had failed them in my leadership. I should have fought more with upper management. I should have communicated the value of these Associates in Barnia to executive leadership. I should have protected them because they weren't in a position to protect themselves (remember the movie A Few Good Men?). I made the ride home feeling terrible, physically and psychologically. I had failed. I had done what the company wanted...**Sidebar: The Barnia announcement was one of the top ten worst times in my life. When my heart began to pound irregularly, I thought I was going to die right there at the meeting.**

Between announcement and exit, the ordeal lasted about 90 days or so. I took the inventory, grappled with the new owners, and went to the closing of the sale. Even though the sale was very successful for the company, the sale didn't feel that way to me. I had always enjoyed traveling down to Barnia to help them out with dispatch, inventory, or other issues that supported the Manager. Barnia is a nice farm town made up of nice farming people. I would bring back fruits and vegetables to the family and they liked the Barnia store too. There were many times when I came back from Barnia and dropped almonds. All of the work and stress that went into the sale and essentially nothing to show for it. Remember this and remember it well. I was watching television recently and became fixated on an interview with Hugh Hefner. You know, the guy who lives with the most beautiful women on the planet in a mansion and shuffles around in pajamas all day. He said the most sticking, striking, "...is that what life's all about?" statement. LIFE IS TOO SHORT TO LIVE SOMEONE ELSE'S DREAM. This statement has haunted me since I heard it. Hef...where were you when I needed that advice a couple of years ago? The man in pajamas surrounded by beautiful women has life figured out. Hef is living his own dream and doing a damn good job of it. Meanwhile, I'm pissing people off in Barnia and having to double-check my fruits and vegetables that I buy at the stand.

MONUMENTAL TASK

On the last day I was in Barnia, I loaded up a bunch of company documents and headed northwest. I was glad to have Barnia in my rear view mirror. A town that I once enjoyed had become the source of almonds and restless nights in the wee hours of the morning. A fellow Associate was following me out of town and radioed me. I thought that he would sing the same hallelujahs I was feeling, but he had something else to report. Unbeknownst to me, papers were flying out of the back of the pick-up truck in rapid-fire succession. The wind was very high that day and the papers didn't stick around for long. The Associate and I pulled over to try and collect as many strays as possible, but efforts were futile. We tied down the rest of the load a little more securely and headed northwest again. I guess I was determined to leave some of the lumberyard behind, and had done so quite successfully after seeing paper strewn across the bean fields. What a mess. The most ironic part of the day was that I had purchased tickets to Motley Crue's Carnival of Sin tour for me and my stepson. As I was coming into Coz, I noticed about eight semi tractor-trailers that were unloading gear for the Crue show at the local arena. I was excited to spend time with my stepson and see a band that I had listened to during my upbringing. Nostalgia has a way of removing the aggravating circumstances of reality. I was very much in need of nostalgia. **Sidebar: I've read the <u>Heroin Diaries</u> by Nikki Sixx (Motley Crue bassist) and it's a great read. Strange how people can reach the pinnacle of their careers and be absolutely miserable (me too!). I think Nikki was not only dropping almonds, but shooting them up as well.**

That was the loudest, most in your face concert I'd ever been to. My ears rang for a week straight after visiting the Carnival, which seemed apropos as my head was aching from the Barnia debacle. Shortly after Barnia, I was instructed to develop a game plan for Nevercan. Nevercan's lease was expiring and the company had no more options. Even though two executive leaders of the organization had a big powwow with the Associates about a year and a half prior, shortly after a competitor opened, and insured them that the company would be there for the "long haul", I would have to travel to the branch in December and let them know that we would be exiting the market at the end of the following year because our lease was going to run out. The whole story was bullshit. The lumber company had acquired the Nevercan branch in December of 1999 and not asked for lease extensions beyond 2006. The lumber company knew in 1999 that the lease was going to expire for the Nevercan location at the end of 2006; the competitor opening didn't even matter.

The Nevercan branch was the most successful branch in the Region at the turn of the millennia. A very strong retail (consumer) base of clients with an adequate percentage of builders in the marketplace. The location made money hand-over-fist. However, because the company didn't know how to manage retail and wasn't interested in learning, the branch was slated for closing in the Fall of 2006. Nobody knew the branch was going to close, other than executive leadership, and they just planned to let the lease run out. There were few, if any, attempts to develop a plan to move the branch out east. All of those half-assed attempts failed and I was left to bat cleanup. Coming out of Barnia and the anxiety linked to that decision, I had learned a few things. I learned that I needed a confidant, a consultant to help see me through some of this mess. Because I believed that no such person existed in the company, I turned to a counselor in Coz to bounce ideas off of. She was a great help and listened to many of the obstacles I was overcoming personally and professionally. The counselor would continue to put me in an uncomfortable place and challenge my thinking and why I continued to make decisions that didn't logically "fit" with me. She was encouraging me to challenge the establishment and feel confident in the decisions I was making. Most things in the world are pretty cut and dry, black and white, and straightforward for us (humans) to understand. Ego and money have a tendency to skew issues and make decisions more complex for everyone. People vying for power and attention have a tendency to minimize the importance of Associates contributing to an organization because their contribution may not support the egos of those in power ultimately making decisions. At the senior leadership level, if someone should disagree in the direction of an organization or a strategy proposed by the business group, the rip tide becomes a little stronger. While executive leadership claims that it's open to the ideas of others and wants the establishment challenged from time to time, talk is cheap. The reality is, at least in my case and I'm sure the case of many others, challenging an organization is viewed as defiant and disruptive to the strategic process. Tensions begin to develop against the cooks developing ideas and those having to choke them down. The Nevercan decision, and all of the crap that came with it, was such an example of a very bad decision.

As I had mentioned before, two executive leaders had visited the Nevercan location shortly after a competitor opened. There was a big rah-rah about how the company was committed to staying in the market long term and that the Associates should stay focused on sales. Mind you, this was about a year and a half before I was going to visit the location and announce the closure of Nevercan. The two executive leaders knew the location's lease was going to expire and they had no interest in renewing. Now, depending how others would spin the story, some may say that the company had every intention of moving the location. Or maybe a last minute deal would be cut with the property owners to extend the lease. The problem I was going to encounter, and this was especially emphasized by the Manager of the branch, is that the two executive leaders had previously stated, "The Company was going to be there for the **LONG HAUL**." A long haul of two and a half years. From the perspective I had and an opinion I hold, the company was using the Associates to protect their position until they exited the lease. The company did not want to disturb operations in Nevercan until the last minute. The problem was complex to boot, the owners of the Nevercan property, by contract, were able to begin marketing the property a year in advance of our exit. So, I was tasked with making the announcement and continuing operations for a year while we closed the branch down. After I assumed the position of VP, I attended a meeting with several other VPs and executive leaders to discuss the Nevercan situation. Some executive leadership was pushing to close the branch down without notice and have liquidators take over. Because that would have only provided me a few months to prepare, I wasn't in favor of walking in and shutting the doors. There would have been serious operational issues we wouldn't have been able to overcome; we wanted to serve as many builder clients through the transition as possible. We would have to find homes for the Associates to be retained and we weren't in a position, with current facilities, to move them to Coz. A simultaneous plan would need to be developed at the Coz branch to receive some Associates and product to be retained by the company. I needed a task force. Not your typical task-force, <u>one that doesn't get anything done</u>, but a task-force of operators, sales, and distribution management that could develop a message and logistics by December of the year I was in. How would they take the news and how would we honor our Associates through the process?

Without getting into the semantics of how decisions were made and why we made them, the most important piece for you to know is when we were going to make the announcement. I picked December 7th, Pearl Harbor Day, as the day for owners and me to get in front of the Associates and look like total idiots. We subsequently scheduled client job-site visits, a meeting with sales reps, and a client breakfast the morning after the announcement to Associates. Several owners, senior leaders, and directors traveled to the market to help us with job site visits.

PRESIDENTIAL ANSWERS

During our sales meeting, Associates from Nevercan and Coz were quite concerned about how we would bring the sales teams together in Coz. They asked several questions and were very insightful to the holes we had in our story. There was a very funny portion of this meeting that I need to rehash. One of our cabinet salespeople asked about integrating the clients from Nevercan and how they, the two cabinet salespeople, would begin to integrate with Coz's sales team. The company's VP responsible for product programs in the organization took a stab at the answer. The guy uses a bunch of words, some of them big and likely from a thick dictionary, but doesn't say a whole lot. You know how the President of the United States uses a bunch of words to give Presidential answers but doesn't say much of anything. The VP responsible for product programs did the same thing to the cabinet sales rep.

He began to answer how programs would be developed to sell product to national builders and how we would have marketing tools to do this, and blah, blah, blah, blah, blah. The guy did everything but answer her question. Whenever anyone gives you Presidential answers, demand more. Don't let them off the hook. They should be able to give you an honest assessment of the situation or simply state that they don't know. If they don't answer your questions, let them know that they didn't answer your questions. By doing this, you'll create an environment of shared accountability. The cabinet sales rep looked at him and stated, "So, you really don't have an idea of what I'll be doing after the transition." I had to step in and save our fearless, almond producing VP. He was doing a lot of hard work to produce absolutely nothing for the Associate. I stated to the cabinet sales rep, "We're very good at giving Presidential answers and it's obvious we're (notice how I lump myself in with an almond factory) not answering your question. The reality is that we don't have all of the answers at this point, but as we develop solutions, we will make you part of that process." The cabinet sales rep seemed appeased when I just admitted we didn't know what we were doing; that we hadn't spent the time to gather all of our facts or solutions to problems that were evident or anticipated. Don't accept Presidential answers. Demand that supervisors give you the honest truth or admit they don't know what's going on. They may come more prepared in the future if they know they're facing a tough crowd.

My boss used to talk himself in circles and I wouldn't bail him out. Finally, he would look at me and say, "I'm full of shit." What a concept. If you don't buy into the bullshit or bail people out of their own bullshit, they realize they are full of shit. Just be quiet and listen intently. Don't try and comprehend it or nod your head in agreement. Look bewildered and continue to listen. It's important that your boss, supervisor, manager, COO, or President understand that you expect and deserve more from leadership. The minute you step in and say, "Hmmm...okay, I understand," or "Wow, it sounds like you've thought this through," you're showing support or indirect compliance for stupid ideas. Don't walk away not understanding your direction or responsibility to the team and your position. Always keep clients in mind and how you will serve them from a change in direction or strategery.

MONUMENTAL CHALLENGES

So, the task force geared up for the big day and developed a list of clients we would visit, invited clients to a breakfast, and scheduled meetings for Associates. We had planned to meet with the sales team first to provide them Presidential answers and prepare them for the all store meeting. The all store meeting would be held in the evening, post close, and all associates were required to be there (duh). The Manager prepared the receiving room for the meeting and acquired a lectern, either for ease of shuffling papers or bodily protection. Associates gathered, either standing or sitting, for the big event that involved ownership and Regional leadership. Maybe they thought we were going to recommit to the previous announcement of the company being in Nevercan long-term and we were going to provide them a road map for their future. I'm pretty good at public speaking, at least I'm told, and I can deliver a good message, as long as the truth is told. I knew there was going to be an obstacle I would need to overcome during the meeting and wasn't quite sure of how I'd handle it until I was put on the spot. How was it that the company communicated one thing a year and a half ago and was changing their position to close the location????????? I knew somebody was going to ask the question, but I wasn't quite sure of how to respond. I would wait until the moment the question arose, and work from the heart and place I was dropping almonds from.

About fifteen minutes into the meeting, an Associate asked, "How long have you known about this?" The correct answer would have been, "Well, the company has known about this since purchasing the location back in 1999. Because the company had no interest in retail and dealing with consumers, they were going to let the property go at the end of 2006. A year and a half ago, when the competitor opened, and two executive leaders told you that we were here for the long haul, well that was a bit of a stretch. We had no intention of staying here long term." Thinking on my feet though, a skill that I've developed over time with savvy parents, I stated, "...I knew about the decision since May and had worked with a team to develop goals for the branch." That seemed to satisfy the Associate and he didn't dig any further, thankfully. I felt bad that I was providing half-truths to cover the company's ass. I could have told the truth and let the Associates know that previous commitments were a bunch of fluff, but I had enough almonds built up already without dropping more.

WHITE LIE

There is a great rock and roll song that captures the essence of white lies and the deception purported by liars. While culturally, white lies may be accepted in mainstream American society, especially business, they have consequences that damage relationships and create mistrust between the people affected. The song, Little White Lies, performed by Sammy Hagar on the Marching to Mars album (Geffen, 1997), provides a glimpse into the lyrical aptitude of Sammy Hagar and his thoughts on white lies. Relationships, whether they are in bands, business, or congregations, are constantly affected by white lies.

Sammy Hagar was publicly pissed at the Van Halen brothers when he exited the band Van Halen. I haven't spoken with Sammy, but I've read enough material to gather Little White Lies was likely written for the Van Halen brothers, predominately Eddie. While Sammy may have been a little miffed at bassist Michael Anthony as well, he likely that Michael would eventually be doomed in the band too. They went on to become the Other Half of Van Halen and toured extensively. White lies haunted the band and created friction between all members. Unfortunately, Sammy Hagar and Michael Anthony were the only band members to represent Van Halen at the very lame Hall of Fame inductions in 2007. So what does all this have to do with dropping almonds?

White lies exist in most organizations. In fact, upon my exit from the VP position in Blunderland, my boss stated to my direct reports that white lies were sometimes necessary in business to protect people. My boss rationalized that telling half-truths to Associates may be better for them. The statement was made during my unceremonious farewell and I couldn't believe my ears. Executive leaders had always touted the company's commitment to long-standing values and how they wouldn't be compromised; yet, my boss, on my last day as VP of Blunderland, explained that white lies were acceptable in some situations. I couldn't believe my ears. I was 100% sure that I had made the right decision to take on other responsibilities. Back to Nevercan...

MONUMENTAL CHALLENGES CONT.

One thing I remember about December 7, 2005 in Coz was that the temperature was -17(f). I rode with a sales leader from the Regional Office in Coz to the Nevercan location. After the meeting was done, I remember looking at her temperature gauge in the SUV and it said -17(f). The temperature was so cold that the LED for the CD player froze; it wouldn't work at all. We were traveling to a steakhouse to meet the owners and other leaders for dinner.

There were two different packets handed out to the seventy or so Associates that worked at the branch. The so called non-essential, retail focused Associates, were asked to work until April 15th of the following year, at which point they would be eligible for a severance package/stay bonus or asked to continue on with the operation's shut-down. The task force believed that five months would be a reasonable period of time to sell through the so-called "hardline" merchandise. The essential Associates, ones tied to builders, were asked to stay until the shutdown was complete or we asked them to transfer to Coz. The essential Associates were also eligible for a stay bonus and pretty much expected to stay. Amazingly, most of the Associates remained on during the phase down of hardline merchandise and eventual close of the store ten months later.

As the VP of the Blunderland Region, I felt like it was important for me to be there for all communications to Associates. I believe there was only one all store meeting that I missed, but our Manager was excellent at providing information to Associates and keeping them updated. Having ten months on my side, I knew that attrition at other branches would assist us with finding homes for key/essential Associates; one of the many reasons I disagreed with some executive leaders about closing the branch in haste. The only problem was, if attrition exceeded the rate at which we needed to close, we would come up short on people at the end, which is exactly what happened. The first round of cuts occurred on schedule in April. I believe that I, with the help of someone from Human Resources, let go of ten or so Associates in mid-April. Most of these Associates were tied to consumer products and the branch had done a good job of selling through them via discounting, sales, etc. The showroom, about 20k square feet in total, was looking empty and the Manager made the decision to bring cabinet and door orders inside the showroom for protection from the elements. I was most impressed with the work of the Manager in Nevercan. I've worked with several Associates during my brief tenure in the lumber business, and the guy in Nevercan was/is exceptional. By far, the hardest working guy I've ever seen, even in the midst of not knowing what his role would be post close. I transferred as many Associates out of the branch as I could find jobs for and a Regional Office Associate and I ended up shutting down the branch. I remember one day in the Fall, a few weeks before we pulled up stakes, I was at the Nevercan location by myself. I was moving racking around and breaking down items to send to other branches. Late in the afternoon with snow on the ground and a chill in the air, I paused on the forklift I was operating for a couple of reasons. The first was that I was stuck in some mud and snow and trying to rock my way out. The second was that a beautiful view was in front of me and I was happy to be alive. The third was that sadness set in, as the branch was so empty. The branch used to be a haven for clients shopping from the north and south along a busy interstate. At one point, the branch was the largest dealer in the nation for a household brand name of products; meaning, they bought more product from the distributor than any other dealer in the nation for one year.

What a shame...what a shame the company couldn't figure out a business model that would keep the branch open and Associates employed. Oh well, my forklift wasn't moving and the day was nearing an end. I also thought to myself, "Self, how dumb are you to be out here on a forklift moving very heavy fixtures around with no one else at the location?" If something tragic was to happen, there was no one around to stop the bleeding. I had emphasized to Associates in the past to work in pairs at a minimum. Here I was breaking my own rules, pissed that I'd been fucking with the Nevercan location for the better part of 10 months, and I wasn't really satisfied with the outcome. Even though the closing had gone well, and considered a success by fellow executives, I felt like I had failed again? Almonds were backing up in my system and I knew that I wasn't doing the right thing. Stress has such an impact on the human body. Linked to diseases of the heart, the digestive tract, and ending millions of marriages, stress was beginning to take a toll on me. I knew exactly what I was hired to do. Not to grow sales, not to improve operations, not to recruit talent from the market and competition, but in my opinion, clean up years of mismanagement and bullshit in a Region that had underperformed since day one.

CONSTRUCTIVE SOLUTION

The company I worked for always-touted "vertically integrated solutions". In fact, there are several companies that tout vertically integrated solutions. When you're in the business world, you will find out that catch phrases and hooks become commonplace in industry. Several companies follow the lead of other competitive companies. There is more time spent copying ideas than developing or innovating new ideas. Therefore, when the lumber industry, housing industry, began to tumble about a year and a half ago, the Pied Piper took most of us to the gutter. There was very little that differentiated our companies in the industry and we all suffered the same consequences. The only companies that didn't suffer as bad were the ones that stuck to a very traditional approach of serving clients. A-1 Lumber, an outfit from the North Pole, didn't jump on strategic bandwagons to take over the world. They continued to focus on service to clients and building upon an already strong foundation of Associates and business principles. They didn't integrate stuff, they didn't acquire much, and they didn't jump on the bandwagon. There is something to be said for a company that sits on the sideline to watch a game of cat and mouse with several other competitors on a playing field.

Well I've bitched, whined, and complained up to this point, so how about some solutions.

SOLUTION #1: MAYBE COLLEGE IS NOT THE RIGHT IDEA

Think about it. College tuitions are outpacing inflation increases to the tune of 2 to 3 times. Because salaries, and the stock market in the past several years, have come up short in subsidizing costs of tuition, parents and students are getting squeezed to come up with funds. While there are several plans, such as the 529, that help parents put coin away for college, most incomes can't provide near enough. Students are taking on debt coming out of college and not finding adequate payroll dollars to help pay off their student loans. Our country in debt continues to perpetuate a problem of higher education costs and student financed debt. And the government continues to talk about the importance of educating children in our great nation?

How about parents? They take out seconds and other equity lines to support the balance they couldn't save. Parents go farther into debt to help support their children's education and end up working longer and harder to pay off debt. Books and meals are put on credit cards and minimum payments become the norm. Need to consolidate your debt? Here's the program for you...

Here's one bit of free advice: If you want to lose weight, quit eating so much. If you want to lose weight faster, exercise while you eat less. No funny gimmicks or diets, just a simple solution to a growing problem in America. **Now, send me the $20 bucks you were going to spend on the book to lose weight fast. Less fuel in the pie hole = less calories to burn.**

Here's another bit of free advice: Save for college from day one. Put money away the minute your child is born. Put as much away as possible, even if it's a minimal amount. Save for eighteen years and see what's available for college and what the remaining debt structure would look like for the student and parent. If the remaining debt structure is manageable, then send the kid to college. If it's not manageable, consider starting a business with the funds. While there will be some penalties and taxes tied to the funds, pull out everything you can to start the business. Work the business with your son/daughter, when possible, and make sure it's something that you and the child are interested in doing.

If you don't want to tie up monies in a 529 or similar plan, then consider basic savings accounts. When the savings accounts have enough money, roll into a CD. The CD option is safer because you'll be less likely to mess with the funds. Because the dollars are post tax, there will be less exposure to penalties and taxation from the government. Even though you will be taxed on gains from the interest bearing accounts, they will be expected and manageable from year to year. There are many financial analysts and money managers that wouldn't agree with what I'm posing, and by all means, they are much more educated in financial matters than me (they rely on your investments for a living too). However, getting a return on investment, albeit college or something else you spend money on, should be very important to you and everyone else in this great nation. Whether or not $100,000 is spent on college or $100,000 is spent on a business venture depends on the student and type of business. Many students drop out of college, look at retention rates, and many businesses fail, look at the lease/for sale signs. Regardless of where the money is spent, both are risky propositions. The question you have to ask yourself is whether or not the value of a business could be long-term and potentially pay for the education of future generations to run it.

I studied psychology and english at the great university of Texas Tech and ended up in the lumber business. While education assisted me getting in the door and communicating effectively with leaders, hard work is ultimately what drove me up the ladder. I enjoyed learning new processes and rolling up my sleeves. I wasn't afraid to make bad decisions and be held accountable for them. How else was I supposed to learn? I jumped at any opportunity to shine and work with peers. No hesitation. No degradation. Just jump in with both feet and get your hands dirty. Regardless of my education, I believe the drive and work I learned from mom and dad would have led to future success. I really would have enjoyed the opportunity to be part of a family business with them. My brother and I would have made a great team and we could have tackled several business opportunities with my parents' leadership. There is much less risk working for someone else, but there is also much less flexibility and equity sharing. As long as you work for someone else, you'll **always** be at risk. Eddie Van Halen, virtuoso guitarist and member of internationally known Van Halen, has been quoted in several sources stating, "He would rather fail with his own music than play someone else's." Mr. Van Halen worked hard to produce his own music and become successful with his own product. I have great admiration for individuals willing to take risks and put their necks out there to succeed or fail with their own products, ideas, or songs in this case.

I'm not sure what the answer is, or what business might be right for you, but consider solution #1: starting your own business with college money for kids as an option. Kids can always return to school and costs may force them to do so anyway. If business yields enough profit for salaries and paying for school down the road, the perfect scenario has played out. Heck, you may be able to write off your own schooling through the business you set up and run. **Sidebar: The United States needs to be concerned about manufacturing more goods for the world and producing more from our soil. We also need to support small business development and entrepreneurialism.**

OLD FRIENDS

One of the most painful circumstances of the Nevercan facility closing was letting go of a cashier. The cashier was an older woman that I admired and came to know after my hire to the company in 2001. She always had a joke to tell and clients enjoyed her style. The cashier had moved from the North Pole facility, when consumer products were cut to the bone, and became a part of Nevercan's team. The move to Nevercan didn't phase her inspiration and joke telling for clients. I had managed this cashier at our North Pole facility and I was happy to see her move to the Nevercan location. My dealings with her as Vice President were mostly in passing and I always made a point to say "hi" or "bye" to her. We remained old friends and I really appreciated her contribution to the store and Region. Very rare the company would find someone in the retail sector that had a good spirit and better demeanor.

That spirit and demeanor changed on December 7th of 2005. In fact, that spirit and demeanor changed for several Associates that were part of the Nevercan location. Uncertainty, even though we all face it, is tough in the professional world. When Associates begin to lose confidence in the stability of a company or leadership of its team, morale drops and productivity wanes. Telling Associates of an uncertain future in the midst of a branch closing poses several challenges, some of which are being captured in the book.

To help the Associates, I didn't bury my head in the sand. Even though I couldn't find a position for the cashier I admired, I found several positions for Associates at other branches. Associates from Nevercan ended up in Barnia, Coz (operations, distribution, and truss management), Enchanted Desert, Mandy Land, and Can'tasia. Some Associates, with experience in providing operational management or builder client services, were even promoted to new positions. All I thought about for 10 straight months was the people of Nevercan, Associates and clients alike. The people were in my hands, and even though I couldn't prevent or change a most certain outcome, I did my best for them.

My old friend, the cashier, didn't speak to me after I announced the closing of our Nevercan facility. She knew she had until April 15th to find other employment, or maybe she believed that she would be retained in some other capacity with the organization. One thing I learned in management up to this point was to not give false hope to Associates as some token form of appeasement. Unlike former leadership, I wanted to face the challenges with Associates and help them at all costs. They were my Associates. I was responsible for their performance, pay, well being, worker's comp, insurance, and all of the other perks that come with having good Associates. While I was disappointed the cashier didn't speak to me post announcement, I understood her disappointment and anger. I accepted her feelings and gave her appropriate distance. I, the company, severed the cashier in April and sent her with a package. The package in our organization consisted of a minimum of two weeks severance and an additional week of severance for each year of service; the cap was set at eight weeks. Of course, Associates, in the company's mind, were entitled to unemployment benefits and the company would not contest the unemployment claims.

That day I let the cashier go, she didn't say anything to me. The haunting disappointment in her face, the reality of what was happening in the office, and the quiet, but quick, processing of her paperwork seemed surreal at the time. Looking back at that day, when the company excused the non-essential personnel, the feeling was surreal. How could we have let things come to this in Nevercan? How did we dump the retail product so fast? Who was going to remain part of the team for the 2nd phase of transferring lumberyard operations? Talk about dropping almonds...I worried so much that I was literally sick. I went to the hospital on July 4th, 2005; my heartbeat had gone irregular during the Batman Begins movie, for whatever reason. My wife and I took our youngest child to the hospital with us while we left the older siblings at the movie theatre. I had phoned the doctor and received the nurse "on call" to explain my situation and ask for guidance. She recommended that I visit the hospital so they could run tests and make sure nothing was serious. The nurse informed me that she would call ahead and they would be ready for me. She wasn't lying. No waiting, no registration, directly to the cardiac wing for tests and I.V. in case procedures should be ordered. I'll never forget what the ER nurse said to me. She looked at me and stated something to the effect of, "You look extremely tense and you need to relax a little (I'm thinking---easy for you to say). Your extra beats are coming from the same place, which is good, but you have to reduce your anxiety." The son that had traveled with us to the ER was getting pretty upset, so my wife called family in to take him home. My wife and I remained at the hospital for four hours or so and I was finally discharged. The attending nurse recommended that I get a good family doctor and consider some anti-anxiety medications to control my attacks. I jumped on a plane the following morning and flew to corporate headquarters with some clients and other Associates. While at headquarters meeting with the clients, my heartbeat was irregular the whole time; at least it wasn't pounding. My life was preoccupied with my next round of irregular beats; very similar to the preoccupation with counting in my OCD days.

My blood pressure elevated to 192/117 one evening during the Nevercan closure, then elevated again on New Year's Eve 2005 prior to guests arriving for a party. I was a mess. I went to my family doctor and asked her for help, I couldn't control my anxiety and knew that it was affecting my health. After a psychological test, I was diagnosed with GAD (Generalized Anxiety Disorder) and put on anti-anxiety medication. I believe the move with the meds saved my life. I noticed results after a month and generally relaxed. Modern medicine is a wonder to be admired. I don't believe that western civilization, at least the people, have managed well in the technological age.
Medicine, information, communication, stresses, etc., have

outpaced evolution leaving a large gap. I'm not sure if our bodies and brains are wired for the absolute bombardment of information and degeneration of family values. Neighbors don't talk much anymore, people aren't so quick to lend a hand to a stranger, and we've all just retreated into our minds and very isolated worlds at home and work. Society seems to be more interested in predictions of the "end" as opposed to the blessings of "new" beginnings. Many people seem to be so obsessed with failure that winning isn't an option. Look at the war in Iraq. Read the papers and then speak with soldiers doing great work over there. Many soldiers will tell you not to believe the papers and that progress is being made in this far away, foreign region to help others. No one seems interested in the progress, but rather the death tolls and how our military has been unsuccessful to control small factions of terrorists in Iraq and surrounding countries. Let's give up, let's fail, let's teach our children to take the easy way out and place blame. Great idea...let's all drop almonds because we read too much into the black and white print of newspapers. It's bullshit; most papers are there to sell advertisements, not newsworthy material. You'll need to go to alternative media sources to get real information and less baked material. Be careful what you choose to believe and the way you assimilate information, as you may become a heretic or pagan worshiper.

THE DAY I TOOK A STAND

By all means, I was completely fed up with my job and performance. I was seeing a cardiologist, seeing a family doctor for GAD, dropping almonds regularly and speaking with a psychotherapist when possible. I'm the kind of guy that loves people and wants to see them succeed, not put them out on the street with very poor explanations for their departure. I was part of a Bacon Lettuce Team (BLT) that was supposed to review opportunities in the marketplace and map out how the company would deploy capital resources to best grow market share. Before doing that, the team would need to look at current resources and how well they were being utilized. A conference call was scheduled to establish new delivery boundaries to better utilize our rolling stock (trucks and trailers). The conference call was to prepare each of the regional VPs for meetings with the BLT. As an aside, when your company begins to develop way too many acronyms for positions in the company, you're in trouble. I remember my boss being very pleased with the acronym development and how we had different acronyms for different responsibilities in the organization. We had MASRs, SASMs, MORs, SBLs, TLCs, OCOs, CECs, SRDs, SCMs, RSCMs, ASCMs, GMs, CORs, RAGs, etc., etc., etc. I remember hearing one executive leader talk about how we should use the acronym for the Associate and not the Associate's name; good idea, let's depersonalize everyone so laying them off will be easier.

The funny thing about the eventual meetings with the BLT was that we, the regional VPs, were supposed to receive a divestiture list (store closing) prior to our arrival at headquarters. The list came at the last minute and I remember a VP receiving his two hours prior to the BLT meeting. I thought I would be in the clear because I had assisted in the sale of Barnia, closed most of the Nevercan facility, was getting us out of our lease from an old manufacturing building in Can'tasia, which had been sitting for about two years, and I had to exit the Mongo facility by the end of 2006 because of lease options expiring. My plate was full, and by the way, at some point, I was going to need to focus on revenue and profitability for the Region. Hard to focus on revenue and profitability when we're closing facilities and moving assets and Associates all over the place. I opened up the divestiture listing and saw Field of Nightmares on the list.

I was shocked. The company had just purchased 5 acres in Field of Nightmares to build a new facility. We had advertised that the "Future Home of so and so company" would be right down the street and sent dirt work and buildings out for soft bidding. How is it that the company would pull out of a market that we had made strong commitments to in the past several months? We also made the same commitments to Associates. They had worked in a run down, piece of shit, converted hotel since the company bought the place. There were like twelve remaining bathrooms from the retrofit and the place was an absolute dump. Forget the Stanley Hotel, the Bates Motel, and any other creepy, horror flick dwelling, the branch in Field of Nightmares was gross. I couldn't wait to move out of the dump. So, what happened, why was Field of Nightmares on the list? How is it that the company could make such a decision? Uh oh, here comes another almond...

Here is how the corporate world works, at least in the organization I worked for, reported to, whatever...The company was courting another lumberyard in Field of Nightmares for purchase. The courting was a period of several months and from what I know, the company was very interested in purchasing the operation. The guy we were courting, the owner, was very much attached to his operation and needed some major coaxing, bullshit, whatever, to convince him to sell to our company. I was even called on by one of the executive leaders to spend a day with the owner to let him know how we operated in the Blunderland Region. I very much liked the gentleman, and to this day, still bump into him. When the deal seemed lukewarm at best, the company I worked for elected to purchase property right down the street from the business we were looking to buy. The move was a gamble, but the company was willing to show the owner of the business we were courting just how committed to the market we were. In essence and my opinion, this was a move to strong-arm the competition. I remember a leader telling me during this whole ordeal that, "If the owner didn't sell to us, we should just pack up and leave Field of Nightmares." I thought this was a little odd seeing as we just invested a million bucks or so in the Field of Nightmares market. Oh well, the gamble was more about business than assets, and the company was looking to take over the top three clients in the market. The retail would have likely been tossed over time, just like in Nevercan. The gamble didn't pay off.

The description of the previous paragraph appropriately depicts what companies say and what companies do. From my vantage point, no consideration was given to the human capital the company had invested in Field of Nightmares. The move, as advertised, was more about market share, or position, than human resource. The company I worked for, a privately held organization with hundreds of millions in sales, was designed to be a political juggernaut, and the company's structure never seemed to disappoint. When I received the promotion in 2005, the company was undergoing a transformation. Ownership had promoted 3 of 6 District Managers to take over newly created, strategic positions at the General Office. The positions were developed to drive the company's future from the General Office. The District Manager positions used to hold the lion share of power in the organization and District Managers were free to manage as they wanted. I'm not sure why the other District Managers were not promoted; I know that one retired during my first year as Vice President and was subsequently not replaced. The owners of the company I worked for did not have seasoned operational experience, even though they held the top executive leadership positions in the organization. There were other family members not involved with the organization that owned shares in the company. There was a Board of

Directors, which used to be comprised of six family members and one non-family member; however, one family member passed away and wasn't replaced, so I'm not sure how the Board voted from that point forward. All of the board-owners were operators in the organization and the non-family board member was as well. Therefore, the company had absolutely no influence at the Board level from outside the organization. Even though, the company spent an exorbitant amount of money on consultants that apparently worked with the top executive leaders. In fact, several of the highest-level executives in the organization spent countless hours with the consultant to develop strategic skills and accountability leadership. Here was the irony involved with the newly created strategic positions...

The VP responsible for strategic leadership didn't graduate from college and had no meaningful experience (my opinion) with strategy and business development. Now, I don't mind people that don't have degrees, and I've worked with several that, in my opinion, possessed better skills of business management and communications than college graduates. However, to put Associates in key positions that have no experience and no formal college education to support a position is problematic. The company becomes a petri dish for bad ideas and strategic thought. The VP responsible for framing initiatives and installed sales had spent little, if any, time working in the world of construction services. While the guy had managed some installed sales (windows, doors, trim, among other things), he had little experience running a framing company or integrating different services under one umbrella. The VP responsible for distribution was very good, but he didn't believe in the bullshit side of our business; he had always been an operator and looked for results to tell the story. Because the company was focused more on implementing missions and strategies, it ultimately took its eye off profitability and revenue growth. My boss at one point told me, "Even if we must sacrifice short-term profitability, we will support the strategic initiatives of the company." In essence, I was doing everything the company asked me to do, but at the end of the day, they wanted the results of short-term profitability. Here's an example...

RED DOT RISING

The Blunderland Region used to finance a red dot program from its Distribution Center (DC). The red dot program was one of a kind, and even though there were objectors in other regions and the General Office, the former VP was able to convince his boss to develop a program of his own. The red dot program contributed at times, 40-50% of the regions overall income in a very strong housing market (1999-2004). The ideas behind a red dot program like this, which are likely run in other companies, are suspect. What the DC would do was this...they would receive carloads/truckloads of product at a certain price and stock units for the branches of Blunderland. There were volume rebates that came with purchasing carloads of lumber into a DC too. Where the program got grey was the DC would charge more for the product to the branches than the costs they received from the vendor. The DC would also trap rebate dollars and hold them for the branch to reconcile at month end. The former VP and the DC Manager would determine how much to trap for the branches at the beginning of the month and review weekly to ensure adequate profit dollars were being trapped. At month end, the DC would make ledger entries to each of the branches, booking back the trapped dollars and dollars received for volume rebates. In essence, the DC would split all of the dollars back to the branches, and would not trap any dollars to cover costs of DC operations. So, the DC was not even a cost center (break-even center), it became a profit center for operations. So, why was this bad?

1. When Outside Sales Representatives (OSRs) were making commission based on gross margin percent, inflating costs from the DC significantly reduced gross margin percents at the branches; in essence, reducing commissions paid to OSRs. From my perspective, pricing from the DC could have been utilized to reduce commissions paid out by the branch/Region to sales representatives. Taxation without representation...remember the Boston Tea Party? How little

some companies learn.

2. Overpriced commodities in the market cause competitive problems when bidding. Work may be overpriced for the wrong reasons. Are truck drivers going to pay $.10-$.15 more for the same diesel they can get down the street?

3. General Managers lacked the discipline to become better managers. They constantly had to call the DC Manager to see how many dollars were trapped for the month. Because they weren't looking at real numbers, there was a false sense of security coming from dollars being trapped.

4. OSRs didn't benefit from receiving higher margin sales. There is excitement driven from OSRs selling more and making more in commission.

5. General Managers/Management Teams made more in bonus because the numbers weren't accurate and were inflated because of the red dot program.

In my first year as VP, I received pressure from several executive leaders to abandon a program the former VP had developed because it wasn't consistent with other regions in the company. To be fair, I felt like the Blunderland Region should perform on the same playing field as everyone else in the company. I explained my dismay in the program of the past and informed all parties that the move would have a "significant" impact on profit for branches along the Front Range. They were all aware of the impact and reinforced the idea that the move needed to be made to be consistent across the company. The Blunderland Region made the change in about September of 2005 and profit dropped significantly. The region immediately lost, on average, about $100k per month in Income From Operations (IFO). The dollars had been moved from IFO to the DC. The VP of distribution wanted to trap enough dollars to cover costs of the DC, which made sense to me. However, by year-end, the DC had trapped close to

$500k in IFO. When I phoned the VP of distribution about an excessive amount to cover DC costs over the past 4-5 months, he explained that he had trapped enough to cover DC costs for the entire year. I explained this wasn't fair to the operators and we should book back excess dollars (compared to DC costs) on a month-to-month basis. I then expressed my concern over the impact this move would have on year-end bonuses. He stated that, "The program hadn't been fair to other operators (other regions) in past years and maybe the company shouldn't have been paying some bonuses to begin with in Blunderland." I thought to myself, "Holy s&*t, this is the true definition of a bait and switch. I've been duped by my own peer group." Here comes the rumbling, the squishy sounds, and another almond. The whole deal was almond flavored pooh-pooh. Welcome to business 101 in the real world. Examples of this type of management are too many to mention here. **Sidebar: The red dot program was a front to preserve profit in the Region. The Region, by my standards, couldn't make money without the red dot program. Unfortunate that the company robbed Peter to pay Paul to protect profits for the Region. The OSRs were penalized, in their pocketbooks, to maintain the essence of a red dot program. Because OSRs were accustomed to selling commodities at certain margins, when prices were lowered in the absence of red dot, the profit was not preserved at the branches. Therefore, most, if not all, of the profit trapped from the red dot program ended up in our clients' pockets through lower prices.**

A STRUCTURED APPROACH TO OLIGARCHY

At the highest level of the organization, there was competition for power and owners' attention. While I'm sure that some jockeying/vying for power was legitimate, most posturing was selfish. Many leaders at executive levels, in all types of companies, are out for themselves and their salaries. Numbers are spun, flaws are overlooked, and an exorbitant amount of time is spent kissing ass and supporting so-so ideas from the top. To make matters worse, very few Associates possess the guts (taters) to tell ownership or the Board of Directors that decision-making processes are filled with flaws. To make matters miserable in the company I worked for, there was no outside representation on the Board of Directors to level the playing field. Therefore, leaders closest to ownership were given unreasonable latitude to force their almonds on the general population of Associates. Because the company I worked for was made up of ownership from two different families, there were loyalties on both sides of the company. Some executive leaders were fond of their favorite family member at the top; while others, in contrast, were supportive of another family member at the top with a different last name. A dynamic developed that was very similar to the Philadelphia Eagles power play between quarterback Donovan McNabb and receiver Terrell Owens. Whose side are you on? Who are you going to support? Who's leading the team to the Super Bowl? In this dynamic, a "chosen one" was appointed to look out for the best interest of owner-operators and shareholders. Because there couldn't be two "chosen ones" to represent opposing families, one rose to the top. Once the structure was put in place, all kinds of committees and councils were developed to flesh out ideas for the company.

The company formed an Obstructive Corporate Officiary (OCO), made up of two owners (different names) and the "chosen one". The company also formed a Bacon Lettuce Team (BLT), made up of several General Office VPs and

Directors, and you guessed it, the "chosen one". I was surprised that the BLT had no field leadership; the "chosen one" was the leader of the BLT. The "chosen one" was also injecting himself in the Strategic Imploding Team and Acquisition/Divestiture teams. Everywhere you went, the "chosen one" was not far behind, ensuring that the company was moving in the appropriate, self-serving strategic direction. As I look back on the past, I realize that there were only a handful of Associates calling the shots in the company, and a majority of those shots were controlled by three people (two owners with different last names and a "chosen one"). The Board of Directors was essentially ineffective at steering the company and councils/committees were established to fill the void, or support the "chosen one". The perfect storm went well beyond the Atlantic...

Remember that whole Field of Nightmares meeting I detailed earlier? During that meeting, I found out that recommendations had already been made to the OCO for divestiture, including the Field of Nightmares location. The deal was done. Do you want to know how it was done? With the wrong numbers from Marketing. There was certain criterion that branches had to meet, or not meet (depending on how you look at it), to be divested. The Marketing Department had made an error in their calculations and had the wrong single-family home starts information for the market. Because they had miscalculated, and the numbers didn't work, I challenged the decision to close based on numbers the Marketing Department had from the first Q of 2006.

The Marketing Department was showing the Field of Nightmares market performing at far better numbers than reality. I queried a member of the Marketing group and showed him that his numbers didn't work, that the branch was performing, according to his numbers, well outside the benchmarks of closing the location. The meeting became somewhat confused and I asked for clarity on the decision. The leader of the meeting, the "chosen one", didn't want the meeting to get weighed down, so he insisted that we press on and the member of Marketing would get me numbers post lunch. The member of Marketing did not return after lunch. In fact, he returned thirty minutes late from lunch with two sticky notes. From the sticky notes, he read the revised single-family home starts for Field of Nightmares. When prorating the numbers for the remainder of the year, the branch came up short to the benchmark of home starts that had been set for divestiture. Boy, what a surprise! Yeah right. Everything was beginning to make sense. From my perspective, the decision to close Field of Nightmares was more based on our unsuccessful attempts to acquire the biggest player in town, not starts. The "chosen one" was getting his way (he had supported closing the location if our local competitor didn't sell to the company) and making the move through appropriate, approved channels, the BLT and **OCO**. I was defiant in the meeting to determine the eventual close of our Field of Nightmares branch because of incorrect numbers and railroading information through the BLT. During the meeting, when I found out that recommendations had already been made to the **OCO** to close the branch, I asked the "chosen one" why I was invited to the meeting. The "chosen one" said that I needed to be aware of the decision and how the BLT would prioritize the closing of Field of Nightmares. I informed the "chosen one" that I wanted to close the branch immediately because I, as well as the Region, were "tired of closing/selling branches". The "chosen one" stated that the BLT would prioritize the closing and provide direction to the field. I reiterated that I was tired of closing stores, the company had a "Future Home of so and so" sign on purchased property, and I didn't want to close a store in 2007.

I obviously made an impression on the "chosen one"; he later indicated to a mutual Associate that "I didn't do myself any favors during the meeting." **Sidebar: Be careful who you tell stuff to in an organization, as it may come back to haunt you and others.**

SOLUTION #2: DON'T DO YOURSELF ANY FAVORS

The "chosen one" was correct; I hadn't done myself any favors. I wasn't going to suck up to a group of peers and executive leadership because I wanted to do myself a favor. I guess I could be agreeable, I guess I could overlook the fact that the numbers were wrong, I guess I could overlook the fact that the company made a commitment to the community, and that the divestiture list came in right at the bell for the meeting. Whenever you're hired on with an organization, be they public or private, don't do yourself any favors. Do favors for coworkers, clients, and trade partners, but be careful about the perception of doing things for yourself. If you're known as a ladder climber or kiss ass, peers will have less respect for you in any position. Give away free tickets to sporting events from vendors, don't keep them for yourself. Some of the things you can do to build a better organization:

1. If you're book smart, leave your books at home. There are several successful business owners and operators that have learned everything from the street. Battles, promotions, and clients are won and lost on the street, not in a Boardroom.

2. When you start with a company, look down before you look up. If no one exists below you, there's plenty of upside potential to your job. As you are training, offer to help in positions with less "glitter". Come in and stock product with the receiving team, work with the sales team to understand their clients, work the service counter to understand how to problem solve while on the phone or in-person.

3. Do the dirty work. Owner-operators of the company I worked for had never operated one of their own branches for an extended period of time. When they made decisions or communicated an idea, their lack of street smarts showed.

4. For God's sake, take out the trash and clean your office every once in a while.

5. Show Associates that you're there to promote them and not yourself. Bring some donuts and a pat on the back every so often to those who aren't appreciated, you know who they are.

FIELD OF NIGHTMARES

I was an expert by the time the announcement was made in Field of Nightmares. I knew the hooks and how to be brief in announcements to Associates losing their jobs. A great quote I remember from <u>Lethal Weapon</u> remains in my mind, "Don't nibble on the barrel, pull the trigger." I pulled the trigger in Field of Nightmares. I had just locked the doors in Nevercan, for good, when I got the news that I would be traveling to Field of Nightmares. Even though the Field of Nightmares branch was not "high priority" in the minds of the BLT, I pushed to close the branch right away. Why? Because I was tired of closing branches and bringing bad news to Associates. I wanted a year, 2007, to be free of closings so the team could focus on performance instead of position with the company. The announcement was quick and fairly painless, much like a seasoned manager firing a so-so employee. Rule of thumb is this: It doesn't get any easier to let people go, you just get better at it. Getting better at it allows a manager to gain confidence to perform a crappy task.

The same blank stares, the same, "what about this or that?", the same general concern for the future. Some Associates, much like the Nevercan situation, transferred to our Can'tasia location. The Regional Office, once again, had meetings with clients in the field. "By the way Mr. Client, the sign that said Future Home of so and so was a bit of a misstatement." And then a big gulp before the next sentence, "Not only are we not building, but we're exiting the market completely." And then you put your best bullshit foot forward, "But so and so is committed to servicing your needs during this transition." In other words, your business is so important to us, we're pulling out of the market.

BUYING YOUR OWN ALMOND

When I was promoted to senior level leadership of the company, I always knew, and even said, that if we began to buy our own bullshit, we were in trouble. The company began to believe its own bullshit, touted it, and marched forward to the future. I couldn't believe some of the things we were doing and saying in the marketplace. We had a bunch of great thinkers that were hell bent on getting attention in the company. Look at me; look at what I've done. "I made an almond in the toilet instead of my training panties!!!!." Me, me, me, I, I, and I. We had some salesmen at the top layer selling bad ideas to the general population of Associates. Most Associates didn't understand the strategic direction to begin with (including me): yet still, newsletters would tout the greatness of top leadership in the organization. Wasn't the newsletter for Associates, and more interesting with Associate stuff in it? The company was strategic now and each of the quarterly newsletters was going to deliver great articles on the strategic direction of our company. Just get out the grape juice and get to drinkin', it's quicker that way.

FIELD OF NIGHTMARES II

We were out of the Field of Nightmares market by year-end 2006. The building was closed up, utilities, at least some of them, turned off, and the lights were shut off. I remember the final episode of Happy Days when I was younger. I believe the cast was in Arnold's, the hamburger joint, and they left one by one. I believe Arnold was left to close up and shut down the lights for the last time. At least this is what I remember happening and that's more important than what really happened. Remember that------------**what people remember is more important than reality**. This is true in divestitures, divorce proceedings, parent-teacher conferences, etc. The less people can remember, the better off you are.

I retained the Manager of the branch for the Regional Office and moved another leader to the North Pole location. Once again, I did my best to retain good Associates for the company. Associates continued to work hard, produce, and make contributions to the team. Even though disappointment permeated the closure, remaining Associates worked hard in the transition to close the branch and move onto other opportunities. I'm still amazed at the resilience of Associates in the midst of bad news and even worse management. Even though there were obvious feelings of betrayal, most Associates maintained a positive attitude through the transition. I was quite pleased to be done with the Barnia sale (2005), the Nevercan closure (2005-2006), the Field of Nightmares closure (2006), moving the Mongo location to Mandy Land, relinquishing a Can'tasia lease back to the owners, even after a copper theft (water lines) caused $40,000 in damage thirty days prior to our exit, and making significant changes to the management team for overhaul and improvement. I'd done everything the company asked me to do and was ready to take a breather from the stormy seas of the Region's past two years. And that's when it happened...

DEJA VU

That's when my boss told me that if results didn't improve over the next six months, he was "...thinking about making a change." I asked him what that change would look like, a question he was not prepared for, and he stated that, "I could return to a GM training program or possibly come to headquarters." A GM training program. Are you kidding me (my middle son says this all the time)? I couldn't believe what I was hearing...

At that point it struck me. I'm just a number in an organization. The hard work, effort, team building, extra hours, and headaches couldn't have saved me from the inevitable. Business is all about looking good, and there was very little I had done in the past two years that looked, smelled, tasted, or felt good, even though it needed to get done. I was looking well into the future and building a team of competent operators to improve our business in the Blunderland Region. I had no idea that I would be excused so early in the game because of something I couldn't control. I thought the owners, Board Members, and peers understood the challenges I had overcome to make the Region a better place. I go back to a statement I made earlier: **what people remember is more important than reality**. I was disappointed that I had missed games, time with my wife, and physically challenged my body in a time of health concerns. My heart burned and burned bright, someday I would tell my side of the story. As I left my boss's office he stated that, "He cared about me." Whatever...my time will come. **Sidebar: I couldn't believe that my boss patted me on the shoulder and told me that he cared about me in light of our conversation. I walked out of that office and left every ounce of respect for my boss in that room. This moment was a turning point for me, a fork in the road, a trial to be overcome.**

Three hours after receiving the crushing blow, I asked my boss for more of his time. I told him that I had considered the proposition and asked him to send me to a manufacturing plant or excuse me from the company. He stated that he wasn't prepared to make a decision and needed time to think things through. My boss also claimed that he made a mistake and didn't intend for his message to come across so harshly. Whatever, I'm done, get me outta here, I can't manage at this level of incompetence anymore. My boss said that he would talk to other team members and work out details of my career move in the near future; the move took my boss about seven months to make.

ALOHA

While aloha means "hello" and "goodbye" in Hawaii, the word definitely took on the definition of "goodbye" for me. Even though executive leadership, including my former boss, knew that I wanted out, they kept me around to take care of more dirty work. They handed me about fifty pink slips to distribute in March of 2007. The company called the move a Reduction In Force (RIF) and I had about twice as many Associate cuts as any other region. So, another plan was put together to perform all of the cuts simultaneously on the same day. I sent leaders out, including myself, to branches to cut more staff. The water-cooler and local pubs became a place of discussion for the mounting uncertainty taking over the company. I performed one cut at the Regional Office that was very painful. I was instructed to cut the Associate because we didn't have similar positions in other regions; maybe that had something to do with the acquisition done in 1999 to buy the joint and the structure that came with it? The lady, a lady I admire, came into the meeting with a notepad to take notes and see what direction the Region was going. She didn't take notes and she was totally caught off guard. Here's the beauty of the situation though. The "chosen one" had an office in Blunderland and one at the company's headquarters. Going back and forth between the offices in Blunderland and headquarters, the "chosen one" made several remarks about me to a mutual Associate that warned of my imminent doom, if I didn't clean up my act of course. The funny thing was, and this is typically how the water-cooler works in business, the mutual Associate would come to me and let me know that the "chosen one" was not pleased with my behaviors, or perhaps, the performance of the Region. Not once did the "chosen one" ever pull me aside to share his feelings or concerns with me. Not once did the "chosen one" give me tips on how to deal with magnitude of problems in front of me. Not once did I feel safe in an office I was sharing with someone on my leadership team. During the time I was cutting the lady I admired, in my opinion, there were inappropriate opinions and perspectives shared by leaders on my team with Associates in the field. Many of those circulating opinions resurfaced in my presence. While I was not a supporter of heresy, there were too many coincidental "actions" lining up with water-cooler opinions. I needed a break...give me a beach, family, and some tequila to clear my mind.

I went to Hawaii in August and was happy to get outta town. Things had cooled down since the RIF and I pressed forward with the remaining Associates/branches in the Region. I made it a point to get out and see more of the Associates during these difficult times. While I didn't agree with many of the decisions, I knew that I worked for someone else. Blunderland is an at-will-employment state, so I could leave at any time and the company could dismiss me at any time. I could have left, but I didn't want to leave. I wanted to see the Region become successful. All of the hard work and casualties couldn't be in vain, I wanted to win. The trip to Hawaii was great and I stayed with my family on the island of Kauai. What a great place and fantastic people. I can see why people sell all of their stuff and leave for Hawaii after they visit the islands. I got totally relaxed. I didn't turn on my phone, look at emails, or anything else work related; and then I came back...

HELP, I HAVE A KNIFE IN MY BACK AND I CAN'T GET IT OUT

I came back to chaos. During my vacation, the company had determined that corporate leadership, six wise men (the "chosen one" in tow), the "Fuck You Bunch" (I heard this description from another peer leader) needed to get involved with underperforming stores. These guys had been through the tough times and the company had survived the Great Depression as well; they were going to save us all from their own crappy ideas and programs. The housing industry had taken one of its worst almonds in recent times and everyone was running around panicking. The company had invested in programs that weren't producing, assets that weren't yielding positive Return On Investment (ROI), and an organizational structure with an expensive price tag. Somebody do something, hurry we're melting, call in the big dogs. That's just what they did in my Region. One of the six wise men invited himself into a meeting with three leaders from the Region to discuss the North Pole location. They began to brainstorm about how to improve the North Pole location. Ideas were put to paper, ideas I subsequently disagreed with, and ideas became action items. I chewed my team out for giving the senior leadership team appropriate ammunition.

I also had a meeting with the Regional team after I returned from Hawaii. The Manager of Mandy Land asked me if I was aware two leaders from corporate headquarters were traveling to Mandy Land on Wednesday for a management meeting. The question was asked in front of other direct reports and I was embarrassed to not be in the loop. My boss had made it clear at the beginning of the year the Vice President, Regional Operations Manager of Wherever was responsible for all of the direction and communication at the branch level. Like most other ideas/programs promoted by the General Office, that didn't last a year either. I was never asked nor told about the meeting from anyone on the senior leadership team. Those guys just went and conducted business without Regional sales leadership and me. I even watched the "chosen one" load up his vehicle and leave for Mandy Land, not a word was said. I sent an email to the two senior leaders and copied my boss to disclose my disappointment in the decisions being made at the upper levels of the organization.

Obviously, I was being unceremoniously shoved aside, and while this did hurt my feelings some, I was already gone. Secondary education doesn't teach you how to handle the politics and management of the business world; universities should teach that in school. Why do we teach our children to believe in things that don't exist? The Easter Bunny, Santa Claus, Tooth Fairy, Great Pumpkin, the entire world flooding back in Noah's time. We are taught to understand the Bible literally from an early age and then informed to take things contextually later in life. Society perpetuates it's own almonds. What about business courses that offer the following: How to fuck your clients? How to convince Associates of something that isn't true? How to sniff out a good liar...In theory, everything sounds great and all of the pieces come together. In reality, Associates at higher levels are more interested in their "own story" and starring in their "own movie". Associates become pieces on a chessboard utilized to protect the queen and king. Pawns are the first line of offense or defense, and they are typically the first to go. The pawns lack the mobility to protect themselves in a game of chess. How ironic that chess is so similar to the business world? Those with the least amount of power and influence, typically the ones that put the most effort into the organization, are the first to go. Get mad or get even, what was I to do?

GET EVEN

At 38 years of age, I believe that I've seen enough to last a lifetime. I wasn't prepared for my first employer going bankrupt twice, prior to folding completely under a Chapter 7. I thought I'd found safe harbor at my next employer, a safe harbor that suffered an oil spill, literally and figuratively. I've cut more people than a training camp with Bill Parcels. I have affected so many people's lives by kicking them to the curb with a couple weeks pay. Some have recovered well and moved on to better opportunities, several have remained disillusioned and displaced. The reality is this: **We spend more waking hours at work than we do with our most prized position, at least most of us do**. Many people make the mistake of investing way too much time in a job that doesn't return the favor. In three decades, the labor market has gone from working a career for life to starting 7 or 8 different careers in a lifetime. Loyalty is a thing of the past and will remain that way until employers value the contribution of basement/ground level Associates.

The only way to get back is to get even. To tell my side of the story with a company that sacrificed Associates and strong business principles to become more strategic and egocentric. Pro athletes are becoming more egocentric, parents at little league games are becoming more egocentric, executive leadership is becoming more egocentric, and politicians have always been egocentric. This great nation, the United States, needs the middle class to survive or else we'll evolve from a democracy to an aristocracy. I have a firm understanding of capitalistic principles and value them greatly, but the spread in salary between educators and athletes is absurd. People need to vote with their dollars and support companies that support their Associates, environment, and communities. Look out for #1 and try not to drop #2. I've been with two large companies that treated Associates like numbers, I'm afraid that my experience is not the exception to the rule. Millions of Associates likely feel this way and it's not good for American business.

SOLUTION #3: LOYALTY

Loyalty is indescribable from a literary perspective. Loyalty for you and loyalty for me has different meanings; however, loyalty can be loosely defined as a commitment to something or a relationship. With the divorce rate hovering at 50% in the United States, our loyalty is faulted from the start. The single most important event of a man and woman's life has a success rate of 50% or less, depending on how you interpret statistical deviation. Couples don't know what they're getting into, the novelty wears off, and everyone but your spouse becomes much better looking over time; add beer and you're in real trouble. The same is true with jobs. You don't know what you're getting into, the novelty will surely wear off, and other jobs take on an attraction that is hard to ignore. Associates begin to think, "The place I work for doesn't give a shit anyway, I'll begin to play the field a little." How funny that our patterns in relationships rival patterns in employment. Some people get so confused over the matter they begin to sleep with coworkers, married and single alike. Misery loves company and you can find plenty at work or home. When we don't get what we wanted or bargained for, we begin to make poor judgment decisions at work. Some of those decisions potentially lead to separation, much like a marriage.

As you enter the labor market, look to make a change, or remain status quo, do us all a favor and lower your expectations. Your boss is human, your Associates are human, and the interviewer that didn't select you is human. There are plenty of mistakes that will be made at your expense. The mistake isn't the problem, how the mistake is handled will define leaders. Own up and take accountability for your actions. For example, the other day I was counseling an Associate with an attendance issue. He could be defined as a quarter horse. He sprints in short bursts, he's the leader in a quarter mile, he plays for one quarter of the game, etc. The Associate doesn't finish well and his absenteeism is causing problems with production.

The reporting Manager was stating that he didn't know how to conduct disciplinary action and keep things somewhat positive. I instructed him to be honest. JUST DO WHAT YOU SAY YOU'RE GOING TO DO. If the Associate's attendance is causing problems to the point of eventual termination, let him know. If the Associate's attendance is disappointing to your expectations, let him know. Just be honest. Don't get emotional, don't make it personal, just let the Associate know consequences of continued performance issues and keep the meeting factual. So many Associates, including the senior leaders I worked with, have a hard time separating emotions from their duties. I mean, who doesn't feel like they're the most important asset to an organization? Lower your expectations to receive better outcomes with peers, direct reports, and supervisors. If you've really mastered the art of team building, begin to hold peers accountable and be open and honest with their contributions, or lack of, to the team. Let's all take off the stripes and become better operators.

As I've developed in management over the years, a competency I've improved is letting go of managing others. While this may sound strange to some, I became a better manager when I began to coach and instruct others instead of intervening in their realm of responsibility. I began to understand that mistakes were part of the learning process, and we (supervisors) became better managers when left to make mistakes and improve. Control freaks don't like this approach, but management caliber Associates will become better as they learn from their mistakes. An important aspect of the "letting go" design is to be present as a coach and mentor. Much of my time in the past couple of years has been spent mentoring others. Part of mentoring others is accepting that some people may have better ideas and expertise than you. If you're fortunate enough to manage others, allow them to become better Associates by letting go. To truly let go, you have to be confident with the mistakes made and problems that surface with the learning process. You will improve as a manager if you're successful in managing the impulse to control others. Teach, coach, develop, and mentor are pretty good principles to manage others in the business world.

I informed the reporting Manager that I was going to demonstrate how to have the conversation. Remain calm, stay focused on facts, and point out something good about the guy. If you can't point out something good about the Associate, you need a pink slip for the meeting. I did just that. Let the Associate know exactly where he stood. No agenda, no backbiting, just a casual conversation about performance and how to improve. I remained calm, shook the Associate's hand, and let him know that continued deficiency was going to cost him his job. Now, I'm not sure if the Associate is honest or trustworthy. I'm not sure if he thinks I'm full of shit (I doubt he does though), and I'm not sure if he'll screw up again, but the bottom-line is this, "I KNOW EXACTLY WHAT I'M GOING TO DO IF ATTENDANCE DOESN'T IMPROVE." In the midst of the conversation, I was creating loyalty between the Associate and me. Even though he might be dropping almonds, I'm not. And the trick is, after all these years, to be the Associate that goes home and doesn't drop almonds.

The business world must create loyalty with Associates to develop, maintain, or go from good to great. Innovations need to occur at all levels of the organization and be recognized. Those Associates on the front lines, in front of clients, need to drive business decisions to help develop a better product for the future. Front line Associates hear comments from clients and establish a rapport that can't be duplicated at higher levels. Associates in an assembly line may have the best perspective of building efficiencies for a product. Sales reps may have the best perspective of an automobile after hundreds of test drives. Is loyalty being created in the organization by opening channels that are free-flowing and move north and south? The company I worked for did not. Information flowed one way from the top; handpicked Associates that drove decisions of the company, some of which were not even qualified to do so. Information did not travel very far north from the basement level, if at all.

ALMONDS DON'T FALL TOO FAR FROM THE TREE

Loyalty begins with family. Family relationships are tested at great lengths to become the foundation of future loyalty for friends, adversaries, and strangers. Let me provide an example. I drove up to the North Pole to visit the branch and take their pulse. The company announced that the branch was closing for performance reasons. Even though the branch had shown promise during the last couple of months, made money, and shown great improvement on the expense lines of the Profit and Loss statement (P&L), the Obstructive Corporate Officiary elected to shut down the branch. With the branch turning the corner, closing down the branch didn't make much sense. Oh well, there was a reason I no longer swam at the top of the organization.

Any-who, I stopped at the local coffee house to fill my cup with a 1/2 leaded and 1/2 unleaded coffee. As I was exiting the parking lot, a big strip mall type parking lot located in everywhere America, there was an accident in front of me. Two cars were approaching me and the one in back became impatient and tried to pass; kind of odd in a parking lot? As the car in back tried to pass on the other car's driver side, the front car decided to turn into a parking space on the driver's side. Confused yet? Subsequently, the car in the back (#2) struck the car in the front (#1) and did some damage. Here's when the story begins. There was a young girl driving the car in front and her father happened to be riding with her. There was a guy driving car #2 with his wife riding on the passenger's side and a very young child in back. After the accident, dad in car #1 immediately exits and gives the guy in car #2 the "what's up" by throwing his hands in the air and pointing at the damage. Guy driving in car #2 exits and begins to yell at dad in car #1. The young girl, probably no more than a few days post sixteenth birthday, exits and walks to the front of car #1. She puts her head in her hands and leans against the hood of the car. Peeking for very brief moments to watch the two animals engage in verbal warfare, she begins to cry. Mind you, all of this happens in about ten seconds. I elected to park in one of the spots adjacent to the accident. I felt loyalty for the young woman.

Because the two men were toe-to-toe and having words with each other, I thought they were going to move from assault to battery pretty quick. Therefore, I walked up to both the animals and very factually asked, "Guys, it's just an accident, but you can both go to jail if you want to escalate this?" I then reminded the father that his daughter was crying on the front of their vehicle and the guy in car #2 had his wife and child to tend to for comfort, injuries, or whatever. The two gentlemen involved in the accident reverted to more primitive behaviors to resolve the issues. They both had insurance, there were witnesses present, and they were still more focused on placing blame. Even with their loved ones upset from the entire ordeal, they were more intent on whooping each other's asses.

The police arrived within three minutes of the accident and began to take over; very impressive North Pole officers to boot. One officer approached me and asked me what happened. I indicated that I was more concerned the gentlemen were going to fight in the parking lot than determining culpability. The officer thanked me and stated that, "You'd be surprised how few people get involved anymore." Even though I wasn't surprised by the officer's statement, I was disappointed to find out that a majority of people would just soon turn a blind eye. We have become a society that would prefer to text message instead of have a face to face conversation, drive by instead of stop to help someone in distress, divorce instead of dig in. While many of you reading this are thinking, "duh, of course the US has become more like this", what are YOU doing to change YOUR actions. The world is only going to get better one person at a time. Almonds don't fall too far from the tree and children will "typically" take on the traits of their parents.

The young lady crying at the front of her car was traumatized, traumatized for life. Her first accident, within four days of receiving the car, would leave her scarred for years. Not because of the accident per se, but because of how two grown men were acting after the accident. Could choices have been different? Could the animals have calmed down long enough to realize the crash was just a minor fender bender? How about checking to ensure everyone's okay? Insurance is just a great big waste of money, month after month, if you don't use it. You are paying for the eventual accident, the eventual fire, the eventual inevitable. Don't be pissed you had the accident, be happy you have coverage to handle it. Look at road rage and people killing each other over shear stupidity. What is the outcome? Everyone is more uptight, more almonds make their way to sewer systems, and people go on the defensive out of the garage. How about just chilling and understanding that people, being human, inherently make mistakes?

Recently, a high school student killed a student, critically injured another student, and dragged his girlfriend to a field and beat her with the butt of his shotgun. The student killed in the altercation was from another school. He had volunteered to take the girl home because other students feared for her safety. The volunteer didn't even know the girl he was driving or boyfriend that would kill him. The boyfriend turned the gun on himself at the end of the altercation. There is no justice, there is no reason for this type of insanity, kids are left to fend for themselves in an otherwise unforgiving world. So where do kids learn this behavior, who will ultimately be held accountable for the crimes? The parents...

Is this fair? Maybe, maybe not. The "maybe" scenario------the parents were aware of the child's behavioral issues and failed to recognize a threat to others. The "maybe not" scenario------local governments have mandated laws that overprotect children from the accountability/punishment they deserve from parents. I'm talking about corporeal punishment. When I grew up, never mind the fact that I walked uphill to and from school in three feet of snow, parents had some latitude to beat some ass. If I stepped out of line, I got a shoe to the head, a punch in the arm, or I was physically dragged from point A to point B. My dad was pretty tough and my mom was very strict. Stepping out of line at home or in school was met with consequences, and some of them were physical. One time during my junior high days, I was sent to the Vice Principal's office and I received three swats with a paddle. The first swat was so hard I couldn't feel the other two connecting with my rose colored cheeks. I tried to stay tough, but man they hurt, and I began crying. I kept crying in the biology class and couldn't let my cheeks hit the seat. I was straddling the seat like some kind of side show rodeo clown. I did something wrong (knowingly), continued to misbehave, and paid a consequence. Kids don't really understand this concept today. Action...reward/punishment...reaction...behavioral change. If schools are allowed to have some latitude with corporeal punishment, within certain guidelines, kids will learn that someone else is there to beat their ass should they get outta line.

While I understand the government is trying to protect children and their rights, social service may be doing more of a disservice in some cases by taking children away from parents. The trauma of a child injuring itself is plenty to handle when rushing to the hospital; to be met by child protective services because of the injury can be catastrophic. Abandoning the principles of corporeal punishment was a bad idea and parents feel less protected to discipline their children. When push comes to shove, parents should be able to kick a kid's ass to show them who has the control. Even if the government put an age limit for beginning corporeal punishment, that would be better than what we've got. Spanking could begin at three years old and a can of whoop ass could begin at the teenage years. Everything should be done in moderation. Don't disable the kid for dumping a plate of dinner on the floor (intentionally), but allow enough force to wake the kid up for accountability reasons.

Parents get tired of having to worry about the boundaries of what's right and what's wrong when disciplining. Kids have this real sense of control that they can turn parents in for mistreatment, which ultimately diminishes the impact of disciplining from parents. So, parents are left to drop almonds because of frustrating circumstances surrounding their children. What can I do, what can't I do? I'll take the safe approach and not do anything. Work has its set of stressors that lead to almond dropping, events at home complicate issues further, and sooner or later you're manufacturing cases of almonds. All of that effort to produce so little product...Be careful how you spend your energy!

SOMEBODY ELSE'S PROPERTY

I've been a stepdad for the past ten years. Being a stepparent is one of the most challenging, rewarding, frustrating, asphyxiating, invigorating challenges I've experienced. Raising your own kids is challenging enough; raising someone else's children can be exhausting. I entered into the arrangement of stepdad several months before my wife and I became engaged. My wife and I knew the minute I met her children I'd be thrust into relationships with them full force. In fact, my wife and I waited six months before I met her children to ensure that our relationship was serious to the point of getting children involved. For couples thinking of melding families or becoming stepparents, I highly recommend that a considerable amount of time be given in the relationship before children are introduced to the equation. Once children are introduced into a relationship through step parenting or childbirth, dynamics of relationships in the family will change.

The step-kids have never called me dad and I never insisted on anything but Bach. The funny, yet sometimes irritating, fact was that my only biological son began to call me Bach and still does on occasion. I've learned that minor details of dad, Bach, or "I hate you" are insignificant to the methods of parenting. I learned a lot of good techniques of how to parent and raise children from my own parents. The almond doesn't fall too far from the tree and we are destined, in many situations, to repeat the successes and failures of our parents. I was not prepared for step-kids, but did my best to become the best father possible to somebody else's property.

Some almonds developed over my own self-confidence and need for approval from my two stepsons. I wanted to be their father, I wanted to be their dad, I wanted to be the guy they remembered as a significant influence to their upbringing and early lives. My own need for approval caused problems between the boys and me. I wanted something they couldn't give me. Not to mention, to ask for something that didn't exist with the children would be unfair in their development. The bottom line is this: I asked for the relationship with their mother and everything, good or bad that came with the relationship. I signed up to become a stepdad for the children through the mother, and that was <u>my</u> decision.

Looking back, would I do it again? You bet. Even though dropping almonds became part of a regular diet with step-kids and a divorcee, I have learned a lot by sticking with it. I didn't bring kids into the relationship and believed, at the time and still today, that a merger of kids from two families would be a design for failure. <u>The minute we have kids, be they step or biological, we stop living for ourselves and begin to live for someone else</u>. If you're not equipped to live for someone else's needs, let alone your own, don't bother bringing children into a relationship. Children don't strengthen relationships, children don't fix issues that exist between couples, and children require much more attention than what we give them today. Because I've always had children in the relationship between my wife and me, I don't know any different.

The most remarkable part of the step-parenting program is that kids have to live with the consequences of relationships. Whether they think I'm a putz, or they haven't enjoyed the experiences of a traditional nuclear family, they live with the decisions of parents. Imagine the almond dropping associated with being a stepchild. The stress of placing blame on yourself, trying to keep all parties happy, trying not to be political, and being sensitive to "how" you spend your time with parents, both real and otherwise; the emotions must be unimaginable. I mean, I was a fucked up kid, mentally, and I came from a traditional nuclear family. I have great respect and admiration for my stepchildren because of what they've endured over the years; and I thought being a stepparent was tough. Stepchildren are little almond producing factories because of the environment they've been introduced to, not an environment they've created. My step-kids have responded very well to the challenges of multiple party parents and are better prepared for the almonds of the real world because of their experiences.

The dynamics involved with multiple parents and households over the years have been interesting to say the least. One thing I've learned, after ten years of experience, is that most parents, biological or not, do the best they can. While there may be varying degrees of "best", and interpretations may differ by individual, most parents do their best based on personal experiences and upbringing.

THE STEADY HORSE WINS THE RACE

This is the best bit of advice you'll ever hear, read, or learn in my opinion. In life, much like in a horse race, the steady horse wins most of the time. I've been to many a horse race and seen horses that expend most of their energy in the first few furlongs, or horses that come from behind a little too late to win, place, or show. Then I've seen horses that are steady with the pack and stay within a few lengths of the leader. Waiting until the final stretch to make their move, horses in the middle of the pack are positioned well to overcome the leader. The horses that stay with the pack seem to conserve energy for the final stretch. Once the jockey determines to let the horse know the race is in the final stretch with the crack of a whip, dynamics of the race change. Some horses fall back, other horses advance on the leader, and the steady horse in many cases emerges from the pack. Of course, horses don't always run the same race, and we don't as humans either.

A good friend, a guy that I met several years ago, is beginning to figure out the "steady horse concept" at 38 years of experience. After two failed marriages, fifty plus jobs, I have no idea how many careers, a drinking problem, and becoming estranged from many family members, he's beginning to figure out the concept of being steady with life. He races everyday in life, and while he may burnout in the beginning or fail to finish at the end in some cases, he has begun to understand the concept of emotional energy and making better decisions for himself. If he makes better decisions for himself, he will be more attune to family needs and issues, and position himself to win most days. If he doesn't, he'll get drunk and blow issues off and not finish a race well. However, just because he lost yesterday, doesn't mean that he's going to lose everyday. Sometimes, because of behavioral patterns and reinforcement, we are more comfortable losing than winning. Maybe we can't handle the demands and pressures of winning all the time. Are we genetically wired to handle the chaos of the world today? Maybe we become stressed and drop more almonds when we're winning. As humans, there is the possibility we need a break from the demands of life on occasion. Some people take a break and self-destruct in doing so. Maybe an affair looks like a plausible answer to the almonds, quitting a job becomes an option, or leaving the family becomes the best scenario; all of these options are irrational to the outside observer, but very rational to the individual caught up in the fray. Many people who are overly impulsive begin to make decisions to set themselves up for failure, because they don't care much for the almonds that drop with winning. My friend went from making six figures per year to living in a storage shed in a matter of a decade. The stresses that came with continued performance were difficult to handle, and the bottle became a reason to crater under the pressure. Yes, drinking is an addiction and very well noted as one. However, why isn't smoking listed as a "disease" with drinking? Because of money, lobbyists, or the corporate influence of tobacco companies? I really don't know. However, I argued until I was blue in the face with my longtime friend. He kept focusing on the disease and I kept focusing on his choices. I encouraged him to start Smoker's Anonymous with me...I digress.

As a youngster I played club soccer in Dallas. The team would travel around the states and, in some cases, out of the country to play at a very competitive level. When I first began to play soccer at the age of five, I loved the game and was quite skilled at the sport. I developed quickly as a player and was scouted by a coach looking to put together a club. I was excited about the opportunity to play at a different level but unsure of the demands placed on players at that level. We practiced a lot and parents were very much into the competitiveness of our league. I wasn't wired to play at that level. While physically I was skilled enough to play club soccer, I wasn't emotionally prepared for the stresses of competing, parents yelling, and being on a stage every Saturday. A game that I very much used to enjoy became a source of almonds and I didn't look forward to playing on weekends. I was more concerned about screwing up than playing the game and having fun.

One night during my junior high days I was out to dinner with my parents. We were talking about soccer and whether or not I was enjoying the sport. My dad sputtered a statement that I hadn't considered up to that point, "Bach, you don't have to play soccer any more if you don't want to." I looked at him and asked, "I don't?" The conversation continued on and I ended up quitting soccer the next day. I wasn't even playing for myself or the enjoyment anymore. I was playing for my parents, my very athletic grandfather, and the image of being associated with a club team (which I didn't much care for anyway). I was relieved. Looking back on this time in my life, trials like these are set at different intervals for us. Most of us fail to recognize them or work ourselves out of them in a productive fashion for family, friends, and key relationships. Therefore, we may consciously or subconsciously set ourselves up to fail to keep our bodies from dropping almonds.

SOLUTION #4: DON'T SIGN UP BEFORE YOU SIGN ON

Whether considering a job, a long-term relationship, a one-night stand, or something that will define your character from this point forward, don't sign up before you sign on. Some people join the military before understanding the demands and travel associated with service. Some people take jobs that pay bills but don't fit their professional needs. If you're heart isn't in the game, don't bother signing up. Find employment that you enjoy and the hours spent away from family won't feel so much like work. Even though I was making sizable bonuses and a pretty healthy salary as a VP, I wasn't happy. I travel less now, made almost every soccer practice for my 6 year old, and I'm happier. My first GM position was in Henderbender. Before accepting the position, I called my wife to ask permission and get her support. We lived about one hour and twenty minutes from Henderbender and the position would require some windshield time to and fro work. My brother lived in Thor at the time, so I would be able to overnight with the in-laws on Monday nights to save some coin associated with commuting.

I pleaded with my wife to allow me to take the position. This was my first opportunity to become a General Manager and I was hungry for the challenge. My wife and I compromised; we probably did that much better back in the honeymoon phase of our relationship. She agreed to let me take the position for a year and then I would need to resign. I thought that was fine and I just wanted the experience to prove myself at a higher level; honestly, today I lack the drive or interest to make that kind of sacrifice. So, I traveled to Store #14 in Henderbender and dug my heels into the branch. After a wonderful, trying, exhausting experience of taking the branch to #14 in the company's overall rankings (200 or so stores), I went to my boss (District Manager) and resigned. I received a bonus for the performance, made sure the check cleared the bank, and went to lie on my sword. I was working long and hard hours, so I hadn't spent the time looking for a new job. The DM asked me if I wanted to stay with the company (sound familiar) and I said, "Sure, I love the company." I actually did. I loved the people, the clients, the goofy sales promotions, and selling. Man, the experience during those days was phenomenal. I truly loved the people I worked with back then and still love them today; many of us stay in touch through work and common friends.

I negotiated a very crappy transfer back to Coz as an outside sales rep. My pay was cut in half and there were 100 or so house accounts that amounted to about $5k in monthly sales that management wanted me to pursue. I relinquished my car and bought a 1976 F-150 that was rusting from the outside in. I hauled everything in that truck. If a client needed product, and the delivery service couldn't get to the order, I took the load myself. The period of three months as sales rep was, by far, the best time I've done in this industry (lumber). I was making very little money but having a ball. At the end of three months, I was covering my draw and making a little commission. However, as luck would have it, I was promoted back into an operation's position in Coz. Some people are afraid to make changes for what changes may bring; however, if people don't take risks, rewards may never be realized. After three months, the house accounts I received doing $5k per month were left doing $5k per month. The business I was able to drum up was new business for the branch. During my time as an outside sales rep I received the best compliment I've ever received in business. I was assisting a custom builder with two speculation (spec) homes and ordering a deck pack for one. We were out back, looking at a beautiful mountain range, enjoying some conversation and probably a dip of snuff when I phoned the order to the branch. After my call, he looked at me and said, "You know what I like about you Bach?" Even though this is taking on the appearance of a tender moment, it's not. I stated, "No." He replied that, "While I know you have 50 or 60 accounts, you make me feel like I'm the only client you have." He wasn't too far from the truth in reality. I had signed on as an outside salesman prior to signing up for the position. Almond free living is the way to go, regardless of income level or notoriety. I had three months sans almonds.

SOME FUNNY STUFF

Van Halen, a band that's reincarnated several times over the past several years, much to my chagrin, has a song called Cabo Wabo. In that song, Sammy Hagar sings about how he's traveled from Rome to Dallas, Texas and man "...he's seen it all." Jon Bon Jovi, another rock-n roll icon wrote a timeless tune with his band appropriately titled, Dead or Alive several years back. In that song, Bon Jovi portrays the struggles of a singer in parallel with a cowboy and tells his fans that, "...he's seen a million faces, and rocked them all." Much like some of my heroes from the hair band days, I understand their experiences. I can relate to having experiences that in some cases are wonderful, and in other cases not so wonderful. I've attempted to rock the Associates I've worked with and show them that someone can be compassionate, motivating, and a disciplinarian at the same time. With those experiences, come opportunities for humor.

Brass Nipples

Very young and fresh outta college (not Compton), I had the world by the horns. I took a pay cut to move from the Biology Department of Texas Tech to the lumberyards of PC. I was so excited to have an opportunity to make a dent in the business world, I really wasn't concerned with what I'd make. I still have the very first paycheck from my first "real" employer. Forget cds, I'm going to be involved in the process of building houses. But oh, the lessons to be learned from becoming street smart. I knew absolutely nothing about the lumber and hardware business. PC also had plumbing, electrical, seasonal, tools, and other builder products. I never built things with my dad and didn't understand the complex processes of putting a Soap Box Derby car together.

PC had an excellent training program that put trainees in a rotation to work all the departments. Because of my total lack of knowledge, I was going to need plenty of time to work my way through the showroom. I started in plumbing. Why not? Almonds flow downhill and check's in the mail. Right? Wrong. In my first week of understanding all that's tied to PVC, CPVC, ABS, copper, solder, sinks, toilets, septic systems, valves, among other things, I learned about **brass nipples**. Now we're talking about something I can relate to! However, a very savvy, good-looking lady shopping in the plumbing department taught me about about brass nipples.

She walked right up to me and asked, "Where are brass nipples?" I should have been fired. I began to giggle like the little bratty fraternity boy I was. After I noticed that she wasn't giggling, I excused myself to ask the Department Manager, who was also a woman, about brass nipples (how embarrassing). The almonds began to back up inside me. Sweat began to drip from my forehead and I nervously queried, "Do we have brass nipples?" The Department Manager said "yes" and they were located in aisle so and so. My heart sunk into my stomach and I wanted to puke. If the customer was a guy, I might have been able to play the circumstance off. Because the customer was a good looking lady, I developed an instant stuttering problem and regressed several million years in intelligence. I escorted the lady down the aisle and discovered what real brass nipples were and how they were applied. Embarrassing moments are key to development of personality and character, as long as we choose to learn from them.

Red Roses

As a very young boy, I had a knack for selling stuff. I remember picking half dead roses with my mom and setting up a rose stand (table and chair) to sell my bounty. Mom thought there wasn't a chance anyone would stop to buy a rose from my archaic stand. I got everything ready, made a sign (with mom's help), and opened for business. I was selling half dead roses for a penny. To my mom's amazement, cars began to pull over in front of our house. In fact, we had to pick more roses to keep the stand going. At one point, a gentleman approached the stand and pulled out his wallet. He gave me a dollar instead of a penny. I didn't know what a dollar was or why he was giving me paper instead of the shiny copper stuff. I later learned that dollars were better than pennies and how many pennies it took to make a dollar. I was rich by my standards. The stand was a success and I got a taste of capitalistic entrepreneurialism. Selling became part of my personality, character, and drive for the future. Who knew I would start with a rose stand? Everyone, at some point, should have the dubious honor of running a stand. Everyone should be required to work in the service sector; we may become more tolerant and nicer to those who serve us.

Shoplifters

The legal system has a way of making life boring. I don't have a problem with the law, but we have too many attorneys, too many laws, too many restrictions, and too many almonds. The land of the free has become the land of overtaxation, driving as a "privilege", court systems that are designed to make money, and protecting the rights of criminals and forgetting the victims on occasion. Don't get me wrong, the United States is the best country on the planet, but we risk losing our position as a great country because politicians are more interested in their own almonds than the interests of the populace. Back in the day, we could tackle shoplifters, detain them, and drag them back to the store to interrogate and have them arrested. When anti-theft devices, a magnetic tagging device utilized to help catch shoplifters, were introduced to the showrooms of hardware stores, life became much more interesting for Associates responsible for protecting the company's assets/inventory. Uprights and alarms were set at exits of the store and alarms would sound when cashiers did not deactivate tags or customers forgot to pay for product. Several times, uninformed shoplifters would buzz right through the exits and the alarm would sound. Some would stop, others would take off.

When the buzzer sounded, Associates on the floor, predominately male, would b-line for the exit in distress. The fun would begin when the shoplifter took off running. Associates of the branch would pursue the suspect on foot and, in most cases, would catch the alleged shoplifter. We could have been shot or stabbed by the alleged shoplifters running from the scene, but we didn't care. Back then, the idea of catching these people was tied more to principle than protecting the company from a $20 loss. As a team, we worked hard and were proud of our efforts to maintain a successful store. We didn't want anybody fucking with our product and disrupting our service to clients. When a member of the team went to sell a power tool only to find that the item was stolen, we all became equally pissed. Not only had we missed an opportunity with a potential client, but we had to write off the item to theft. Was there pent up anger existing in the team from items that were being stolen? You bet. Did we take this out on alleged shoplifters we caught? Sometimes. The treatment of the alleged shoplifter was proportionate to the cooperation they gave us.

One time I caught a lady shoplifting and took her upstairs to the office and called the police. With the door open and keeping an eye on the woman, she pled with me to let her go because she had nothing on her possession from the store. She was full of shit and I knew she was full of shit. However, she proceeded to take her clothes off in defense of her position. She pulled her pants down to reveal her underwear and I immediately stopped her. As politely as I could, while sneaking a peek, I asked her to keep her clothes on until the police arrived. If she had nothing, she had nothing to worry about and could prove her case to the police. She calmed down and waited for the police to arrive. She was arrested for shoplifting and issued a citation.

Another time I chased a suspect until he dumped the product. An Associate and I were in pursuit of an alleged shoplifter that apparently forgot to pay for a bunch of tool accessories. The salesperson in the department indicated the suspect had been over in the tool accessory area and wahooed (taken) a bunch of packages. Small drill bit accessories come in tiny packages that are very easy to conceal and toss in coat pockets. This guy had plenty and he was quick like a rabbit. As we pursued him through some commercial buildings adjacent to the store, he tossed a majority of the product into some juniper bushes. Because the Associate and I were not in the best of shape and the product was dumped, we stopped pursuing the man.

We had so much fun pursuing the alleged criminals testing the security and ability of the team at the location. Then things began to change. People started suing for wrongful detention and other goofy laws utilized to protect criminals. Granted, innocent people shouldn't be treated like criminals; however, innocent people don't have much to worry about. Businesses became afraid of lawsuits and didn't want to risk exposure in the media for mistakes. Therefore, shoplifting became much easier and Associates were encouraged to "not" get involved.

Advice from my attorney...

Because of legal advice and living up to the disclaimer at the beginning of the memoir, I had to edit out, completely, a section of the narrative that was tied to a bizarre experience of the past six months. Some sections will be left for consulting.

My Humps

I recently started a DJ, sound system, and live music company named DJ Bach. Anywho, the business takes me to some cool locations and I meet thousands of neat people. During 2007, our band Caliente Chorizo, was invited to play a wedding reception in Silverado. The road trip was great and we really enjoyed attendees of the reception. The reception was celebrated at a lodge at the base of a mountain that had a "bunny hill" ski lift. The lodge had wrap around decks and there was plenty of room to enjoy a cocktail and the most spectacular views in the world.

Some of the younger crowd was getting trashed and they had very eclectic tastes in music. I did my best to download several requests for the wedding party prior to the event, but I couldn't cover the tastes completely; the band was mixing live music with iTunes. Establishing the boundaries of taste in music, I elected to go out on a limb during a break and play a little hip-hop for those in attendance. I brought up the Black Eyed Peas on my laptop and selected My Humps for the next tune.

Shortly after the introductory horn section announced a forthcoming bum-pity-bump, a young lady appears out of nowhere. She looked pissed and in her bitchiest voice asked, "**What's that**?" I immediately replied, "**My Humps**". Being somewhat pissed and frustrated, the young lady retorted, "**I don't like My Humps**." With a quick quip and a penchant for good humor I explained, "**Well I don't like your humps either**."

There's nothing like hanging with people getting loaded, dancing, and listening to great tunes. I've had so much fun with DJ Bach, maybe some day I'll turn the business over to one of my sons.

The Log Ride

My first summer job was at a theme park in Arlington, Texas. During my high school days, my parents always made sure that I was employed by spring break. Because I had no experience and immediate value to the theme park, they placed me in food services and I was assigned to a lemonade stand at the exit of the Log Ride. The Log Ride has always been a favorite of guests attending the park in Arlington, as temperatures during the summer would exceed 100 degrees on a regular basis. Guests of the park would get drenched by the water ride and were eager to quench their thirst with freshly squeezed lemonade.

The lemonade stand also carried pretzels, popcorn, nachos, and cotton candy to wash down with lemonade. I really enjoyed working with the crew at the lemonade stand and generally enjoyed management that supervised our employment. I very much valued my employment with the theme park and respected the way they treated Associates of the park. However, there was a very important **lesson** I learned at the lemonade stand.

There were two windows at the lemonade stand and cash register stations set up at each. A guy by the name of Mike and I were responsible for tendering transactions and balancing the cash drawers. There was an assistant, someone I viewed more as a supervisor, who made the lemonade, prepped the food, and oversaw operations to ensure the stand ran smoothly. The only issue we ever had was with Mike's cash register.

Mike followed protocol and reported several issues with the register to operations. The buttons would stick, the register would seize, and Mike would become frustrated because guests would have to wait while he worked through the issues. I can't remember if the park sent out a technician or if the complaints were filed by phone or in writing, but Mike's register continued to give him issues. The register gave us issues until one very busy weekend day.

Mike and I had about 5-7 guests in each of our lines. The assistant was cranking out lemonade and getting all of the food orders ready. We were moving through the orders until Mike became completely frustrated with his register. Mike was frustrated because the piece of equipment was preventing him from excelling at his job, Mike was frustrated because he had reported the problem on several occasions, and Mike was frustrated that the register was still failing. At that point, something very bizarre happened. Mike, very calmly, went over to the counter that housed the lemonade dispenser and other pieces of equipment for the stand. He reached under the counter and lifted a 5-gallon bucket of dish soap. By my estimates, there was probably a gallon of dish soap left in the container. Without pause, Mike raised the jug over the cash register, positioned the spout over the register keys, and began dumping dish soap on the register. After the register sputtered and went dead, Mike returned the jug underneath the counter and retrieved some towels. I'm not sure what the guests were thinking in Mike's line, but they must have been in awe of his brazen act to finish off the register.

Mike phoned the operations office to report that his register was dead, apologized to the guests and informed them that his line was closed, and began to wipe soap from the register with several towels (he cleaned it up very nicely). I went from having 5-7 content guests in my line to 10-12 guests that were becoming somewhat aggravated. At first I thought the scenario was hilarious, until all of the guests moved to my line. **Sidebar: If Associates are asking for equipment and tools to help them perform their jobs, do your best to meet their needs. If equipment should fail or begin to fail, don't try and save a buck by waiting until equipment fails completely. I have always remembered Mike's cash register for this reason. I felt that if I didn't take care of Associates' needs and assist them in performing their jobs, they might leave the team or fix things themselves.**

SOLUTION #5: HOW'S YOUR PORTFOLIO?

As you look for a job, help yourself to not drop almonds in the midst of an interview process. I learned from my debacle with a record company and discovered a thing or two about the interviewing experience. My first real opportunity as a Showroom Manager came at the beginning of 1994. The company (PC) had just undergone a restructure, one of many, and regions changed landscape with regard to boundaries and bosses. My contacts in Dallas disappeared overnight and I was left to become familiar with a new set of leaders. I had done customary schmoozing, as a Trainee, in Dallas and positioned myself well with regional leadership and key executives. The world I was living in changed overnight and I had to acclimate myself to a new environment. Shortly after the restructure, an opportunity became available in Coz for the Showroom Manager position. I was the least qualified and tenured person interviewing for the open position. Because of my previous interviewing experience with a record company, I had tasted the role of underdog and wasn't going to leave myself exposed to the elements of interviewers. I began to ask my peers and leaders what I could do to become a frontrunner and secure the position. **Sidebar: Even though the record company pounded me during my first "real" interview, the interviewers taught me a lesson: Don't take a knife to a gunfight. I appreciate the interviewers doing what they did, or else I wouldn't have grown in my experience.**

I had read my interview book and looked to the guidance of those with a history of interviewing for direction. One gentleman, an Operations Manager that I valued tremendously, developed the idea of a portfolio of items I could discuss during the interview. The portfolio would complement the resume, and I would have pictures, timelines, and success stories to share based on my experience as a Trainee. Not knowing what brass nipples were the year prior, I would need to convince local management in Coz that I knew my shit and could lead a very tenured, successful branch.

The idea of a portfolio was constructed to help me stay on task during the interview and not get sidetracked based on my lack of experience. I was going to be interviewing against Associates with decades of experience and I didn't have the benefit of pulling from multiple sources of knowledge. My years and age were going to work against me, and I needed to overcome those deficiencies prior to the interview process.

I needed to make the most of my limited experience and chronicle the items in a binder. I began to take pictures of items that I developed for sales ideas, safety concerns, and marketing promotions. I focused on aspects of my training program when I was able to be entrepreneurial and share accountability with the management staff. I was building up pages and pages of pictures, sales figures, and promotional ideas that I'd been part of at the branch. With the help of an excellent teacher, the Ops Manager, I put together a very professional binder of my experiences during the past year. I had done mock interviews and been tested by some very good interviewers prior to my flight to Coz.

As luck would have it, a huge snowstorm hit the Coz area and shut down the airports. I was scheduled to leave early in the morning and return during the evening of the same day. There were delays at the Armadillo airport and weather was atrocious to the northwest. Because the flight was running behind, I approached the lady at the counter to see about the status. She informed me that, "...the ground crew is topping off fuel in case the plane should need to turnaround and come back." I didn't feel great about the news, considering the plane was a small, one seat each side, prop job. When boarding began, I got a case of the butterflies. After getting on the plane, I got a case of the "Oh shit, what am I doing!" Boarding the plane didn't feel right and I got off. I informed the counter that I was not going to fly today and needed to book a flight for the following day. The airline was okay with rescheduling and was probably pleased to get me off the plane (more weight for fuel). I'm not sure if the plane ever flew that day. **Sidebar: I**

was scared out of my mind getting on the flight to Coz. In fact, I was so scared that the hairs on my arms were standing; I believe this called piloerection in the medical field.

I immediately called my boss and the District Manager slated to interview me in Coz. I made them aware that I was unable to fly today and would reschedule a trip the following day. The District Manager in Coz acknowledged the weather was poor and to travel safe the following day. I was met with better weather the following morning and eager to arrive in Coz for the interview. I needed to redeem myself from the record company interview and trained myself like a prizefighter in the Russian Alps getting ready to fight the heavyweight champion of the world. I had my portfolio in hand, a business suit cleaned and pressed, and the confidence I would need to overcome objections from the interviewers. The only thing I didn't have was an overnight bag, which is a mistake if you're traveling to Blunderland on a plane during the winter.

I arrived for the interview and waited in an office adjacent to the interviewing area. I believe someone may have been interviewing, but I was more involved in studying work history and knowledge acquired over the past year. After what seemed like an eternity, the lumber manager retrieved me from the office. He escorted me to the interviewing area and I met the District Manager with a smile and firm handshake. We began our conversations with the customary bullshit of talking about the weather and flight to Coz. Flying into Coz with the snow-capped peaks was the most incredible site I'd ever seen. I couldn't believe how pretty the mountains were with terra cotta colored faces and a tree line beaming with some of the most beautiful greens I'd seen. The picture was perfect and I was living in my own postcard.

The interview went very well. I had anticipated the gentlemen would hone in on my one year of experience and the fact that I was much younger than the "seasoned" Associates I would be managing. I was prepared to speak to my weaknesses by accentuating my strengths. I pointed to opportunities where I had overcome age differences, knowledge gaps, and a general lack of experience in the business. I would substitute my lack of knowledge with hard work and dedication to understanding the positions of those supervising the store. I didn't emphasize that I had a college degree, I didn't emphasize that I was going to be an assistant in the very near future, and I emphasized that I never quit learning during my training process. I took everything I could and wrapped it up into a portfolio to take the position.

I went to the portfolio very early in the interview, with the hopes that the gentlemen would become preoccupied with what I'd done, as opposed to what I hadn't. The interviewers were very good and focused on specific situational questions such as, "Tell me about a time when...", or "You mentioned a time when this occurred, how did you handle the situation with Associates?" If you're with a really good interviewer, they won't ask questions that are subjective. They will stick to specific situations that support your resume, experience, and portfolio. The best indicator to tell if someone is lying, or fudging their experience, is to ask specific questions about such experience. There have been several situations when I've interviewed an individual to find out they're inflating their experience. I immediately strike individuals from the hiring list and cut the interview short when I can tell the interviewee is misleading the process. Getting back to the overnight bag------I got snowed in the afternoon of the interview and couldn't fly out until the following morning. **Sidebar: Thanks to United Airlines for putting me up in a room for the night near the airport. The Samaritan at the counter forgave my inexperience and stupidity.**

Some of the things you should consider for the portfolio:

1. Specific details regarding your experience, preferably tied to positions that dovetail with the job you're interviewing to win.

2. Pictures of neat things you've done or manufactured during your experience. These can include product ideas, merchandising techniques, and sales events that you helped manage.

3. Sales figures tied to product ideas and promotions. Show your results and show them clearly. If you successfully reduced loss with inventory at a location, provide specific details of how you accomplished an objective (#1) and improved the results in doing so (#3).

You don't want to make the portfolio so complex that a cursory review would lead to confusion. Appealing to multiple interviewers and managers in business, put visual examples in the portfolio, put statistical information with graphs and charts in the portfolio, and put brief summaries together of your experience that relate to the position you're interviewing to win. Don't overburden the interviewer with TMI (Too Much Information). Remember, the portfolio is a supplement to your speaking ability. If you become uncomfortable during the interview with your speaking ability, you can always retreat to the portfolio and provide examples of greatness. Is the portfolio a crutch? You bet it is. Will the portfolio help you win a position and outclass others? You bet it will. Trust me, I've been through so many boring, redundant interviews hearing the same story provided by candidates for a position. Those applicants that are creative getting in the door and keeping my attention will typically win approval. If applicants are innovative and creative during the interview process, they will likely be during the time in position too.

SO, WHAT IF I'M AN ALMOND DROPPER?

I'm a dropper, she's a dropper, he's a dropper, they're a dropper, wouldn't you like to be a dropper too? First and foremost, you're in good company. All of us, at some point in our overly stressed and eventful lives, become almond droppers. While some of us drop more almonds than others, we all drop almonds. The trick to almond dropping is to drop them as infrequently as possible. While inevitable, almonds are manageable from a stress and lifestyle perspective. First idea:

FAMILY

Where you at in your family situation? If all is not well on the family front, you're very likely to have problems outside the home. During my brief tenure as a counselor and 30 some odd hours of graduate school, I saw my fair share of almond factories. Family issues bled over into career issues almost 100% of the time. Your family needs to be in order and life becomes less complex from there.

Children may get the wrong ideas of what's important in life based on the decisions you (parents) make. When my parents first went to counseling in the midst of my OCD, the psychiatrist asked them both, "So what's going on with you guys?" Even though my dad felt everything was fine between my parents and they didn't need counseling, the psychiatrist stated, "He (me) is just acting out, you guys (parents) may very well be the source of the almond." My dad took offense to this but my mother understood the approach from the psychiatrist.

My mother had struggled with her own issues and alcohol dependency during the latter stages of college and the introductory period of her marriage. My mom was also committed to making herself, and better yet, the family a **working** unit. Thank God she understood what the psychiatrist was talking about because I was a few almonds away from the nut house. My mom and I worked together in counseling and discussed some very tough topics. She would work with my dad on their issues and they became a stronger couple, regardless of whether the effects of the work were evident back then. My parents worked very hard on their relationship and I respect my father for stepping up instead of stepping out. The easy decision for my father to make would have been to start over with someone else perhaps. My dad endured years of dysfunction with his own parents and became a very successful businessman and father; like many other fathers of the 70's, probably a little more successful as a businessman.

The only drawback to much of the attention being focused on me was that my brother was glanced over with regard to his own issues. While my brother's issues weren't psychiatric, the attention on me was inequitable. I resent myself, to some degree, for putting my brother in an uncomfortable place, but I didn't know how to overcome my problems. If this book is dedicated to anyone, my brother deserves the recognition for not receiving the recognition he deserved during the early stages of our development. Instead of wallowing or playing the pity party, my brother went off to college, graduated, has a great family, and is a Vice President of a very large company. He has done quite well, under much more difficult circumstances than me.

Family is about sacrifices and what we can do to contribute to the greater good of the organization. Much like business, if part of the family is not on board or contributing to the whole, a family will ultimately suffer. If one or both parents are cheating, issues will manifest themselves in the family, not the relationship. If one of the children is lying excessively, issues will manifest themselves in the family. Nothing is isolated in the family and nothing is off limits. Kids should not be allowed to make decisions, as minors, that may endanger the family unit or themselves. If they are drinking or drugging excessively, they need to be confronted. If children become combative, remind them who's paying the bills and who has leadership in the family. If they don't care who leads the family, show them a little "**labor love**" or the door. Get rid of them if they don't appreciate your efforts. Don't ever let male children disrespect the mother without severe consequences. Don't ever let female children disrespect the father without severe consequences. Have I muscled my step-kids around a little bit? You bet. Do they respect my wife and me? You bet. They may not like me at times, but they will respect the family.

Kids---understand that your parents are far from perfect and you ain't going to be much better at the parenting program. You can learn a lot from your parents, and to this day, probably have. Placing blame on others is such an easy scapegoat to the reality of today's issues. As I mentioned earlier, **Do what you say you're going to do and be honest.** If you get caught with booze or dope as a minor, fess up and take the heat. If you're doing crappy in school and parents approach you, let them know that you haven't been living up to your end of the bargain. I have worked with my middle stepson for years to help him be honest and assume accountability for his actions. He was such a piss poor liar and kept on looking for opportunities to escape his consequences. Night after night, consequence after consequence, he kept on getting punished. He finally figured out that consequences would be less severe, if any, should he tell the truth out of the gate. Him and I had plenty of moments when we would be in line at the toiley to drop almonds. He didn't give up and I didn't either; thankfully, our relationship is much stronger today.

CAREER

Are you really that important? I've been at the top of an organization and can tell you, without a doubt, you're not. Companies will continue to chew through Associates like a wood-chipper after a windstorm. You're not as important as you think you are, and there is always someone out there that believes you should be performing better. So, what can you do?

Get your priorities straight to prevent the almond dropping that comes with careers. Family first, career second. I'm not sure if the Gen Xers, X Boxers, Play Stationers will have the same problem as my generation or the baby boomers. They have seen their parents get laid off, shift in careers, have duel incomes, and all of the other stuff that comes with chasing the American Dream. I've never been enamored with the idea of sacrificing moral principles for the sake of money. I struggled with my role as a VP and became aware that my ability to whack others and cut expenses made me more wealthy or appealing to executive leadership. How self-serving is that? Many executives are paid huge salaries to produce poorer results. During my tenure as VP, executives stayed in tact at the top as field personnel were massacred with lay offs. In fact, as the field was cutting personnel, the General Office was adding directors to corporate layers. What kind of message did that send? People were amazed that high dollar personnel were being added to the General Office as we cut low cost laborers. The structure put in place to do $1 billion dollars by the end of 2010 yielded half that; yet, there have been relatively few, if any, cuts at the corporate executive/director level. The company **replaced** me and a VP of Sales that was booted for more acrimonious reasons.

If you're really comfortable with yourself, just wait until your company sells to a parent or you get new management in place, especially strategically minded leadership. Your world will turn upside-down several times as you pursue the greater good of capitalism. Don't get too hung up on one letdown or a missed opportunity, there are several around the corner. Remember, the steady horse wins the race and your ability to serve a family far outweighs the ability to serve a master.

As baby boomers retire, there will likely be a shortage of available labor in the market, especially for those industries serving baby boomers. If you want an "almost" sure thing, train for the medical field as an assistant or nurse. The pay is good and the supply of nurses is challenged nationwide. Many analysts are predicting that demand will outpace supply as baby boomers retire, which may save the bacon of our new, high-tech X-Boxers.

Be careful whose ass you kiss. If you're kissing ass from your level up, you're kissing in the wrong direction. You really need to take care of your peers and direct reports. If they like you, advocates at lower levels of the organization will outnumber the leaders at the top. If you're impressive to those you serve at the field level, you will be impressive at the top end of the organization. One of the principle reasons I was not terminated from the VP position, especially after being somewhat defiant, is because I have a pretty good following of Associates. I have assisted Associates with job placement and career development all throughout my tenure in the industry, and I will continue to do so regardless of my position in the industry. Remember this, in the midst of an organization's blunderful management, Associates will become more loyal to each other. Associates coming together to create their own teams, in the absence of corporate leadership, are good for relationship building, but not good for the company. Senior leaders, at some level, will begin to lose their significance and power with Associates when this dynamic occurs. In the company that I worked for, the power shift occurred and senior leaders retreated to their offices. Not knowing what to do, they chose to do as little as possible or nothing. Communication became erratic at best and usually non-existent. If you've put too much faith in the leadership of others, and ultimately your career, almonds begin to drop on a daily basis, if at all (constipation). You become more backed up than the George Washington Bridge with an accident during rush hour. When you put faith in others (humans), you run the risk of becoming highly disappointed when they become egocentric and look out for themselves.

Work hard and put in a reasonable day. If you're working too many hours, let's say more than 55 in a week, you're obviously not managing time or subordinates well (that is if you have any). A reasonable amount of time to get things done in a week is somewhere between 40-50 hours. By all means, take the time away from work to enjoy kids' activities and their interests, or your own hobbies. You will be a much better parent if you take the time to enjoy your children. Enjoying children at the early stages of development may keep you from spending an exorbitant amount of time with them during the teenage years. A balanced career = a balanced family life.

FAITH (Optional)

Here's the tricky, million dollar question: to believe in a higher power or not? Many hemorrhoidal almonds have been dropped over the issues of Christianity, Islam, Jewish, Buddha, Mormon, and countless other faiths that believe in people, cattle, and the extraterrestrial. Faith is a very personal choice and one that we all encounter at some point in our development. To keep society from dropping almonds and give peace a chance, here's a bit of advice:

BE MORE CONCERNED ABOUT YOUR OWN FAITH THAN THE FAITH AND DEVELOPMENT OF OTHERS.

People will seek out faith when they need it; don't forget that we're somewhat selfish as human beings. Because of life's circumstances, the need to give thanks for blessings, or protect a country (sect) from outside influence, people turn to religion during times of need. Religion (organized faith folks) brings people together for very noble or not so noble causes. The interpretation of what's noble is left up to the eye of the cleric. Whether an individual is performing mission work in the Sudan or electing to chase the Hale-Bopp comet, nobility is left to those following. Leaders need followers and followers can choose whether or not they drink wine or poisoned grape juice. Faith is really up to the individual and people can decide to lead or follow.

What I don't understand is why people spend so much time dropping so many almonds to convert other people to their religion. We all have a choice to make, or not make, with regard to faith, and we will ultimately follow our hearts (for those who have them). If people are non-believers, that's fine; if people are believers, well that's fine too. I am a believer and after my health and career issues, I felt there must be something greater than what we see. I couldn't take advantage of others, so I was left to putting my faith in the hands of a higher power. I was baptized Presbyterian and raised mostly Catholic. Even though I haven't been made official to the Catholic church, I'm a practicing Catholic that takes communion and attends church with my family. My wife was raised Catholic, married in the church, and obviously divorced; that is, if you've been paying attention throughout the narrative. She never received an annulment from the Catholic church and remarried me in a Methodist church. Because she hasn't had the marriage annulled, there are problems with her marrying me and kids being involved. To be quite honest, I'm not even sure of what those problems were or are to the Catholic church. I'm not sure if God cares, but I can tell you I don't. Rules become very hard to follow in the Catholic church and I'd just soon go attend mass not worrying about what I haven't done or need to do. How can you be at peace when you feel guilty about not giving enough, getting a marriage annulled, or not living up to certain churchly expectations?

LET US PRAY...

I was attending Catholic mass and very much into the homily (sermon) and messages of the priest. To some degree, I was mesmerized by the moment and not thinking about what I was doing. Catholics are always sitting, standing, and kneeling depending on what part of the mass you're participating. The priest was about to read a passage from the Bible and motioned the altar boy to his side. As the altar boy opened the bible, the priest raised his hands and sang, "Let us praaaaaaayyy." Being somewhat in the moment, I sang out, "Ookkkaaaay." There were a few people around me that had to notice my blunder in the presence of God, even though they didn't lead on with looks or whispering. My wife began to giggle and we still laugh about the moment today.

I began giving several thousands of dollars to the parish for the school my youngest and middle sons were attending. I felt like, because I was making good money, I needed to share the wealth with a great principal and staff of teachers instructing my children. The school had been on the bubble for a few years because the diocese had too many parishes/schools within a few miles of each other. The bishop had made his way out a few times to conduct meetings with the school's parents and faculty. A finance committee had been established to advise the bishop on options and impact studies to keep schools open, or close them down. I had been impressed with the school for several years and glad to have my son attending a place of study and worship. In the spring of this year (2007), I wrote a check for a sizable sum of money to the school (enough for one student's annual tuition '07-'08). I spoke with the principal and let him know that my wife and I were happy to contribute to the school and very satisfied with his leadership. Little did he know that the financial committee had already met with the bishop, advised the school be closed, and let the staff, students, and families fend for themselves.

I believe we heard news the school would close the week before summer vacation. The church "family" of students and faculty was devastated by the news. Many parents frantically enrolled students in other Catholic schools, some parents didn't relocate to other Catholic schools, and some merely disappeared. The student body was absolutely crushed that years of instruction and dedication to a school were wiped away in a matter of days. The Principal was not aware of the decision until the last minute; therefore, teachers were left to find jobs at the tail end of the school year. Kinda strange how the human side of religion boils down to dollars and cents. I'm not quite sure why priests live a life of celibacy and are so committed to living their lives in the likeness of Christ. At the end of the day, they are just as human as you and me. Some of these flaws are evident in the Catholic church and others are likely more subtle. How many almonds must these people drop to try and live above humanity? There is only one son of God and that's Jesus Christ, and while living a life like Christ far exceeds nobility, I believe it has to be next to impossible. Only Christ, the son of God, can accomplish the miracles and passion above humanity. I don't quite understand the whole dynamic, but I believe the Catholic church needs another Vatican Council to dump the goofy hats, the uniform, and celibacy. Just my opinion, but what do I know. After the school closed, the money we had provided for scholarship ('07-'08) and teachers' funds never resurfaced. I'm not sure where the money went, but I hope they used it for intended purposes. People all over this nation have experienced the story I'm telling, and the almond I'm dropping. Maybe we should lower the "bar" for what's tolerated and not tolerated in churches today.

Faith is really up to you and whether or not you choose to believe. Outside of believing or not believing, we still have responsibilities to act in accordance with what's morally right. If we all believed in each other a little more, we might be surprised at how Christ like we may become. Until society figures out how to prevent inexplicable murders, the solicitation of children, hunger, and wackos on the Internet preying on all kinds of people, a higher power is going to be pretty unimpressed with humankind as a whole. How about, in the United States, if we just committed to helping citizens of the United States first and everyone else second? We have people in our own country that are suffering emotional and physical pain that can't afford the help they need. How about if every tax dollar goes to United States' programs first, including our first class military, and we provide the leftovers to the world? Just an idea...

I will continue to put my faith in a higher power because I don't have much faith in humankind. One of the most relevant quotes I've heard came from the Terminator himself, Arnold Schwarzenegger, in the movie <u>Terminator II</u>. He's leading John Connor, the adolescent boy, around with his mother and trying to protect them from terminators that have been sent back from the future to kill them. When John Connor asks his protector why the world will come to an end as they know it, Arnold, in his very thick Austrian accent responds (something like the following), "It's in your nature for you to destroy yourselves." Very true and very enlightening coming from the Governor of California. Until we can overcome the nature for humanity to destroy itself, we will drop infinite almonds.

Faith is a choice, and if you choose not to decide, you still have made a choice (Rush/<u>Freewill</u>)...Sidebar: The band Rush has some of the most profound and provocative lyrics of rock-n-roll. From songs like <u>The Trees</u> to <u>Freewill</u>, Rush has entertained audiences with their music and lyrical prowess for several decades.

Here is a recap of some of the solutions up to this point:

SOLUTION #1: MAYBE COLLEGE IS NOT THE RIGHT IDEA

SOLUTION #2: DON'T DO YOURSELF ANY FAVORS

SOLUTION #3: LOYALTY

SOLUTION #4: DON'T SIGN UP BEFORE YOU SIGN ON

SOLUTION #5: HOW'S YOUR PORTFOLIO?

LIFE SANS ALMONDS...

Is there life without almonds? As long as we have people and politicians, absolutely not. However, your goal in life should be to reduce the output of almonds your body is producing. How does that happen? Look deep inside and understand your passion and needs in life. If your busy work schedule conflicts with family time, consider making a change to fill a need. I hear all the time, "I wish I had more time to spend with family." The reality is that people make an active choice to not be with family. Another reality is that spouses cheat and people lie on a very regular basis. Finally, we have become a society that glorifies professional athletes and violence. We all make choices to impact our societies. As long as corporations and people chose to pay 80 bucks per ticket for sporting events and spend twice that on booze and food, society will value professional athletes more than teachers. As long as Associates choose to pour 70 hours of work into a week and neglect their children, we will have dysfunctional families. As long as people chose to do drugs and spend their money on mind-altering agents, the United States will be a leader in the world with drug use. Many people, whether they realize it or not, contribute to the almonds of others.

I'm committed to helping **individuals and organizations** reduce their almond output. While you shouldn't necessarily "learn" from my experience, you should be aware that Corporate America can be vicious to those with conscience. I was very ill prepared for executive leadership and the callousness that comes with being a Vice President. Many companies, in my opinion, are out to serve themselves and the top of the organization. There are a few companies that truly embrace Associates and maintain long-term relationships with their human capital. Statistics reveal that people will experience multiple jobs and multiple careers in their lifetime. With baby boomers retiring and workforce supply dwindling over the next several decades, we may see a retroactive shift to companies looking for long-term relationships with

Associates. Until then, be mindful and aware of your surroundings. A company that treats Associates well is destined to treat their clients well. Those companies that embrace changes long-term will surely position themselves well with human capital available in the marketplace, those that don't will likely find themselves competing at a disadvantage.

HAPPY TRAILS

Dropping Almonds is my maiden voyage for writing a memoir. I hope that my accounts of Blunderland and being involved at the executive level of a company will help you understand the dynamics immersed in upper management and decisions made at the highest levels of an organization. Experiences that led to my almond dropping are likely similar to the experiences of millions of workers that endure the nature of corporate America today. You don't have to be at the top to understand the dynamics of an organization or how decisions affect coworkers and clients.

When I first embarked on this adventure, someone asked me, "Why don't you write your story in the context of fiction like many other authors?" After thinking about the question, I responded that, "These are my experiences and the issues I've encountered at the highest level of an organization for the past couple of years." While I could mask the essence of my story by writing about fictitious people and places, I would lose information and emotion in translation. Therefore, I elected to hide identities, places, and committees within the text, including my own identity.

Where do I go from here? Much like I mentioned in the previous paragraph, I want to assist employees, managers, and executive leaders with taking a good hard look at themselves and how they interact within a team. I've been through many sessions with strategic consultants/advisers and left feeling a little empty. The reason I always felt a little empty is because I usually thought we skimmed the surface of our "real" issues/problems. Leaders must be torn down in order to press forward as a team. If anyone on your team, at any level, thinks they have business figured out, you might want to follow them to the latrine. You'll likely find they're dropping almonds.

To my mom, one of my biggest heroes, I'm sorry about all of the shit references throughout the memoir. However, when I look at the business world and all of the almonds that come with it, what goes in will eventually find its way out.

Map of Blunderland

● North Pole   ● Nolava

● Nevercan

● Mandy Land

● Mongo   ● Enchanted Desert   ✸ Coz

● Field of Nightmares   ● Can'tasia   ● Barnia

www.ingramcontent.com/pod-product-compliance
Lightning Source LLC
Chambersburg PA
CBHW051723170526
45167CB00002B/781